GROWING in CHRIST

40 Days to Deeper Faith

ARNIE COLE &
MICHAEL ROSS

© 2015 by Back to the Bible.

Print ISBN 978-1-63058-367-5

eBook Editions:
Adobe Digital Edition (.epub) 978-1-63058-965-3
Kindle and MobiPocket Edition (.prc) 978-1-63058-966-0

The authors are represented by and this book is published in association with the literary agency of WordServe Literary Group, Ltd., www.wordserveliterary.com.

Published by goTandem, an imprint of Barbour Publishing, Inc., P.O. Box 719, Uhrichsville, Ohio 44683, www.barbourbooks.com

Our mission is to publish and distribute inspirational products offering exceptional value and biblical encouragement to the masses.

ecpa Member of the
Evangelical Christian
Publishers Association

Printed in the United States of America.

Contents

JESUS IS THE DELIVERER AND REDEEMER

JESUS IS "THE WAY, THE TRUTH, AND THE LIFE"

JESUS IS "GOD WITH US"

DAY 1:

A RIGHTEOUS MAN

"Joseph son of David, do not be afraid to take Mary
home as your wife, because what is conceived in her is
from the Holy Spirit. She will give birth to a son, and
you are to give him the name Jesus, because he will save
his people from their sins."
—Matthew 1:20–21

→ SEE HIM

Joseph of Nazareth—Redefining Honor

He isn't rich by any means, yet life is good for Joseph.
He enjoys working with his hands—building, creating,
shaping, pounding. His trade as a carpenter keeps him
busy, and the future looks bright for this upstanding Nazarene. A smile stretches across his face as he smoothes the
rough surface of a wooden door he has made. Once put
into place on his neighbor's house, the oak barrier will be
sturdy and reliable for years to come—much like Joseph
himself.

*Sturdy and reliable—a righteous man who keeps the law
diligently.* This is the kind of person Joseph was raised to be.
After all, his family can trace their ancestry back to King
David.

But Joseph has a new reason to live up to his family's
proud heritage. He has given his heart to a beautiful young
lady named Mary. (A big wedding ceremony is in the
works.) Joseph imagines the countless memories Mary
and he will share as husband and wife: hearty meals by a

crackling fire, endless talks late into the night, the laughter of children—lots of children. Joseph dreams of filling his home with sons and daughters!

Then one day, his dreams are crushed.

"Mary. Oh my beautiful Mary. What's wrong? You seem different somehow. Happy, almost glowing—yet frightened as well."

His bride-to-be blinks away a tear and lowers her head, placing Joseph's hand on her abdomen. Mary looks up again and meets his shocked expression with an uneasy nod.

Yes. There is a baby in Mary's womb! But how—why?

Joseph pulls his hand back and quietly leaves. Distraught, he walks aimlessly through the village. He eventually comes to his house and steps inside. Joseph latches the door behind him, curls up on the floor, and begins to weep.

How could this happen? How could she betray me this way? There's only one thing to do: release her from marriage. She must wed the father of the child.

Strangely, though, Joseph feels no rage, only a great disappointment that settles like a permanent knot in his chest, weighing him down and making it hard to breathe. How could his judgment be so flawed, so far from the mark? He had looked forward to marrying the young woman whose character and temperament had made her seem all the more likable.[1]

Joseph wipes the tears from his eyes and drifts off to sleep. Suddenly, the voice of an angel calls to him in a dream.

"Joseph, son of David," the angel says, "you should not fear to take Mary home as your wife, because the infant conceived in her is of the Holy Spirit. She will bear a son, and when she does you must call his name Jesus, since he will save his people from their sins. God is fulfilling prophecies, Joseph!

" *'Behold, a virgin shall conceive and bear a son, and his*

---

1. Ann Spangler and Robert Wolgemuth, *Men of the Bible* (Grand Rapids: Zondervan, 2002), 318–19.

name shall be called Emmanuel.'

"Emmanuel," the angel says. "Emmanuel, God with us."[2]

Then Joseph wakes up and does exactly what God's angel commanded in the dream. He trusts the Lord, even if it defies common sense, even if it threatens all of his well-laid plans and hopes and dreams, even if it means ridicule and shame and being misunderstood by others. He knows that this is one special child growing inside Mary.

So he takes his bride home as his wife, but he does not consummate the marriage until she has the baby. Then he names the child Jesus.

→ HEAR HIM

Explore the Word: Matthew 1:18–25

Mary's pregnancy put Joseph in a desperate position: How could he uphold his integrity and reputation when his fiancé had become pregnant?

He planned to divorce her quietly, which in that culture would have been gracious, sparing her and her family from terrible disgrace. From all Joseph knew at that point, Mary had committed adultery, and according to the law, the penalty was death for her and dishonor for her family (see Deuteronomy 22:13–21). To understand how offensive Mary's pregnancy was, we have to examine ancient Jewish culture.

The Jews had a special custom for couples getting married. Before they could marry, the couple would enter an engagement period called a "betrothal," which would normally last about one year. After the waiting period, the couple married and only then joined together in sexual union.

But this betrothal differed significantly from modern engagements. Once a man and woman were betrothed, everyone considered them as good as married. Although

---

2. Walter Wangerin Jr., *The Book of God* (Grand Rapids: Zondervan, 1996), 588.

they reserved sex for marriage (after the betrothal period), people called them husband and wife. Only death or divorce could dissolve the bond. They couldn't get "cold feet" or date around to find a better mate: they had essentially gotten married.

One of the purposes was to see whether the couple would remain faithful to each other. If the woman got pregnant by another man, thus breaking her vow to her husband, he could legally divorce her for her offense and make a public mockery of her for her sin.

Joseph discovered Mary's pregnancy. What would he do? His response shows his true character:

Joseph listened to God. He heard what God planned to do through Mary and the Child she bore. Yet to follow the instructions given, Joseph had to do more than just listen.

Joseph believed God. He could have laughed at God or blamed his strange vision on the previous night's matzo balls. But he believed. He didn't have to take Mary as his wife. He didn't have to call the boy's name Jesus. But he had heard the message and believed it as true. How do we know he believed?

Joseph obeyed God. He did what God told him to do. The scriptures purposely use the same language to describe both what God commanded and what Joseph did. What did God tell him to do? He said two things: "take Mary home as your wife, because what is conceived in her is from the Holy Spirit. She will give birth to a son, and you are to give him the name Jesus" (Matthew 1:20–21). And what did Joseph do? When he arose from his sleep—he didn't put it off for weeks, but acted immediately—he "took Mary home as his wife," and when the Son was born, "he gave him the name Jesus" (Matthew 1:24–25).

The Bible tells us something else about Joseph's righteous character: He "kept [Mary] a virgin until she gave birth to a Son" (Matthew 1:25 NASB). Imagine getting married and waiting a few months before having sex with your wife! But Joseph placed preserving God's ways above fulfilling his own fleshly desires. There would be no question about the source of this child—the Holy Spirit.

Joseph displayed his righteousness through listening, believing, and obeying God. Perhaps he experienced gossip from some, ostracism from others, yet he did not compromise his integrity. His example set the standard for all who strive to be people of honor. Authors Ann Spangler and Robert Wolgemuth write this in their book, *Men of the Bible*: "During the formative years of the Messiah's childhood, Joseph lived a consistent and exemplary life of faithfulness and obedience to God. Imagine how important it was that Jesus grew up with a father whose character was worthy of emulating."[3]

Do you want to be an honorable man or woman who has a reputation for godliness? Set your eyes on the character of Joseph, one of the true unsung heroes of the Bible.[4]

→ Know Him

• **Listen when God speaks—and trust His Word.** Despite what some people say, the Bible is more relevant than ever. It teaches us how to live in peace with others, stay out of debt, and persevere under pressure. Most importantly, Scripture teaches us how to grow closer to God. But for it to affect us, we have to listen to God through His Word and believe what He tells us.

> ✳ *Work It Out: It's a good idea to get in the habit of asking ourselves questions daily: What is God saying to me today? What has God already told me that I know I need to obey? Pray without ceasing? Keep my mind and my body pure? Add to this list. Share some other questions that we should ask ourselves daily.*

• **Obey God—even when nobody's looking.** The Lord keeps us in His sight, and He looks favorably on those who

---

3. Spangler and Wolgemuth, *Men of the Bible*, 323.
4. A portion of this devotional lesson was adapted from David Barshinger, "Father of Jesus," *Breakaway* (December 2004), 27–28.

walk with integrity. If we want genuine faith, we need to follow Joseph's example and put faith into action—obeying the Lord in public, as well as when we're alone. So, if the Lord tells you something through His Word, such as, "flee the evil desires of youth" (2 Timothy 2:22), do you claim to obey in public, then make excuses in private? We often struggle to obey God, but active obedience confirms true faith.

✳ *Work It Out: Which statement best describes your faith: (1) A solid rock on the shore, battered by the elements, but stable in Christ. (2) A wave of the sea, blown and tossed by doubt. (Please explain your answer.) Read James 1:2-27. Based on this passage, name some steps everyone can take in order to build a stronger, more authentic faith.*

• Pray: **"Lord, help me to be a person of honor like Joseph."** Ask God to enable you to honor Him with your words, your actions, your life.

→ NOTES FOR GROWTH

A Key Point I Learned Today:

_____

_____

_____

How I Want to Grow:

_____

_____

_____

My Prayer List:

_____

_____

_____

DAY 2:

GOD CHOOSES MARY

When Elizabeth heard Mary's greeting, the baby leaped in her womb, and Elizabeth was filled with the Holy Spirit. In a loud voice she exclaimed: "Blessed are you among women, and blessed is the child you will bear!"

— Luke 1:41–42

→ SEE HIM

"He Will Be Great and Will Be Called the Son of the Most High"

Mary rushes to her cousin Elizabeth and Zechariah's place, which is about sixty-five miles away (not exactly an afternoon stroll). Elizabeth is upright and blameless before the Lord, but infertile and well along in years. She has all but given up on ever having a child—until her husband, Zechariah, received some amazing news in a most incredible way.

Zechariah is a priest and the direct descendant from the first high priest of Israel, Aaron. One day, an honor of a lifetime came to him as he served at the temple. As part of the liturgy, he was selected for the sacred assignment of burning incense to God.[1]

Suddenly, an angel of the Lord appeared to him, standing at the right side of the altar. When Zechariah saw him, he was startled and was gripped with fear. But the angel said to him: "Do not be afraid, Zechariah; your prayer has been heard. Your wife Elizabeth will bear you a son, and you are to call him John. He will be a joy and delight to you,

---

1. Leith Anderson, *Jesus: An Intimate Portrait of the Man, His Land, and His People* (Minneapolis: Bethany House, 2005), 10.

and many will rejoice because of his birth, for he will be great in the sight of the Lord. He is never to take wine or other fermented drink, and he will be filled with the Holy Spirit even before he is born. He will bring back many of the people of Israel to the Lord their God. And he will go on before the Lord, in the spirit and power of Elijah, to turn the hearts of the parents to their children and the disobedient to the wisdom of the righteous—to make ready a people prepared for the Lord."[2]

Zechariah recovers from his fright and asks for proof since he is an old man and his wife is past her child-bearing years. The angel's answer surprises him.

"I am Gabriel," the angel says. "I stand in the presence of God, and I have been sent to speak to you and to tell you this good news. And now you will be silent and not able to speak until the day this happens, because you did not believe my words, which will come true at their appointed time."[3]

As Mary and her cousin meet, Elizabeth's unborn baby leaps for joy as Elizabeth is filled with the Holy Spirit and calls Mary the mother of her Lord. Elizabeth tells Mary how fortunate she is, not because she has done anything on her own, but because she has simply taken God completely at His word and trusted Him.

Mary agrees but makes sure the glory goes to the right Person. She praises God for choosing her, for His love that encourages the humble, and for the fact that what's happening isn't a new plan but the fulfillment of an ancient promise.

Here's what Mary says—her poetic words mimicking the style of Old Testament prophets she heard quoted in the synagogue:

> *"My soul glorifies the Lord and my spirit rejoices in God my Savior, for he has been mindful of the humble state of his servant.*

2. Luke 1:11–17.
3. Luke 1:19–20.

> *From now on all generations will call me blessed, for the Mighty One has done great things for me—holy is his name.*
>
> *His mercy extends to those who fear him, from generation to generation.*
>
> *He has performed mighty deeds with his arm; he has scattered those who are proud in their inmost thoughts.*
>
> *He has brought down rulers from their thrones but has lifted up the humble.*
>
> *He has filled the hungry with good things but has sent the rich away empty.*
>
> *He has helped his servant Israel, remembering to be merciful to Abraham and his descendants forever, just as he promised to our ancestors.*[4]

Mary stays with Elizabeth and Zechariah for three months—the remainder of Elizabeth's pregnancy. And when delivery day arrives, everyone is pretty excited when Elizabeth gives birth to her son, John. But the neighbors can't quite swallow the name: "What's with John? Listen, don't you know the firstborn is named after the father? That's how Jewish people keep the family name going. There's not a single John in your entire family!"

But Zechariah isn't about to make the same mistake twice. When the angel Gabriel first told him that he would be a father, he didn't believe it so his speech was taken from him. The angel also said to name the son John—which is exactly what Zechariah would do!

He writes in no uncertain terms, "His name is John." And because of this act of faith, he immediately begins to speak and prophesy about coming events.

---

4. Luke 1:46–55

→ HEAR HIM

Explore the Word: Luke 1:39–80

She's young, poor, and relatively unknown—and yet God plucks her out of the crowd and raises her up to help change the world. The gentle and lowly Mary of Nazareth has three qualities the Lord values: genuine piety, profound humility, and unfaltering holiness.

Mary first conceived Christ in her heart by faith, before she conceived in the womb, and the testimony of Elizabeth both expresses and stamps the whole character of the Virgin: "Blessed are you among women, and blessed is the child you will bear!"[5]

Born like the rest of women in sin and shaped in iniquity, she had her human faults and needed a Savior as others did—"My soul glorifies the Lord and my spirit rejoices in God my Savior" (Luke 1:46–47)—but the witness of scripture is that in circumstances of unparalleled responsibility she exhibited a true and godly character, and in spite of any weaknesses she may have had, she was "the most pure and tender and faithful, the most humble and patient and loving of all who have ever borne the honored name of Mary."[6]

→ KNOW HIM

• **Mary learns to trust.** A virgin birth? Almighty God coming to our rescue as. . .*a helpless infant*? The King of Kings born of a peasant maiden? Mary has good cause to feel skeptical, but instead of doubting she simply says, "I am the Lord's servant. May it be to me as you have said." We, too, would be wise to trust God with our future, with our very lives. We can embrace the promise He made to Jeremiah: " 'For I know the plans I have for you,' declares

5. Herbert Lockyer, *All the Women of the Bible* (Grand Rapids: Zondervan, 1967), 94.
6. Ibid.

the LORD, 'plans to prosper you and not to harm you, plans to give you hope and a future' " (Jeremiah 29:11).

✳ *Work It Out: Does God have your complete trust? Are you willing to believe, even when the assignment seems impossible—and the future uncertain?*

• **Mary stays focused.** Have you ever met a person who seemed perfectly centered, focused, and at peace, even when the rest of the world seemed to be falling apart around them? More than likely, that person's mind, heart, and spirit were centered on God. Mary was one of those people. Today, we live in an unsettled, tumultuous time in a world full of strife, suffering, pain, and grief. Despite this, inner peace and stability are possible, even in turmoil. When our hearts are in tune with God and we are focused on His work in and purpose for our lives, we can proceed steadily and courageously through even the most painful circumstances. Peace *is* possible, and it begins in Him.

✳ *Work It Out: Think about how you can learn to keep your focus—even when life doesn't make sense. Will you give up your personal desires and embrace God's plan for you?*

• **Pray: "Lord, please guide my heart and mind toward You so that the kind of peace that transcends all circumstances is possible through You."** Ask Him to help you battle doubt and learn to trust Him more.

→ NOTES FOR GROWTH

A Key Point I Learned Today:

_____

_____

_____

How I Want to Grow:

_____

_____

_____

My Prayer List:

_____

_____

_____

DAY 3:

IMMANUEL ARRIVES

*"Today in the town of David a Savior has been
born to you; he is the Messiah, the Lord.
This will be a sign to you: You will find a baby
wrapped in cloths and lying in a manger."*
— Luke 2:11–12

→ SEE HIM

The Birth of Jesus

It doesn't seem like a suitable place for the King of kings:
the animals, the filth, the smells, the flies, the dusty scratchy
hay—and having a feeding trough, of all things, for a crib!
But God, in His infinite love, chooses the humblest possible surroundings. No one can accuse Jesus of not knowing
hardship and pain.

As Mary studies the face of her baby, she isn't just
looking at a precious child; she's peering into the face of
her Lord—His Majesty. Mary knows she's holding God in
her arms. *So this is the One the angel told me about.*

She remembers what the angel had told her: "You are
to call him Jesus. He will be great and will be called the Son
of the Most High. The Lord God will give him the throne
of his father David, and he will reign over Jacob's descen-
dants forever; his kingdom will never end."[1]

But at this very moment, baby Jesus looks like anything but a king. His face is reddish and prunelike. His cry,
though strong and healthy, is still the helpless and piercing
cry of a baby.[2] And He is absolutely dependent upon Mary
for His well-being.[3]

---

1. Luke 1:31-33.
2. Max Lucado, *God Came Near* (Portland: Multnomah Press, 1987), 23.
3. Ibid.

The sky above the manger is torn open with a multitude of the heavenly host praising God and promising peace on earth to those who please Him: "Glory to God in the highest heaven, and on earth peace to those on whom his favor rests."[4]

As the angel choir withdraws into heaven, the sheepherders talk it over. "Let's get over to Bethlehem as fast as we can and see for ourselves what God has revealed to us." They leave, running, and find Mary and Joseph, and the baby lying in the manger. Seeing is believing. They tell everyone they meet what the angels said about this child. All who hear the sheepherders are impressed.[5]

Meanwhile, Mary remains as obedient as ever.[6]

→ HEAR HIM

Explore the Word: Luke 2:1–20

Two things strike me (Arnie) as I read this passage:

I can't help thinking about the stigma of being an unwed mother in the early Jewish culture. Imagine the angry stares and cruel remarks from those you once thought were friends. In spite of the fact that Mary's world has been forever altered in extraordinary ways, she remains committed to God's plan.

Second, it's not to the kings, or to the great intellectuals, or even to the celebrities that God sends the ultimate birth announcement. Instead, the Creator of the universe first shares His great joy with simple, humble shepherds. (Apparently high positions don't impress Him very much!)

Are our eyes fixed on God's faithful love? Can we see beyond our own problems and experience His love—just as Mary did? If you're having trouble with that, keep in mind

---

4 Luke 2:14

5. See Luke 2:15–18, MSG.

6. A portion of this story was adapted from Bill Myers and Michael Ross, *Faith Encounter:Experience the Ultimate With Jesus* (Eugene: Harvest House Publishers, 1999), 16–17.

that part of His love involved coming all the way down to our level to live in this dirty, sin-infested world in the person of His Son. Let's move in closer and get a better look at this Son. . . .

No beauty. "He had no beauty or majesty to attract us to him, nothing in his appearance that we should desire him" (Isaiah 53:2).

No reputation. The Bible describes Jesus as one who "made himself nothing by taking the very nature of a servant, being made in human likeness" (Philippians 2:7).

No sin. "God made him who had no sin to be sin for us, so that in him we might become the righteousness of God" (2 Corinthians 5:21).[7]

→ KNOW HIM

• **Meet the God of wonder.** "For unto us a child is born, unto us a son is given. . . . His name shall be called. . . Wonderful" (Isaiah 9:6 KJV). Even now He is working in just as amazing ways as when He created heaven and earth. Our challenge to you in the days ahead: Strive to get the full picture of Jesus and be attracted to Him with new *awe* and new *wonder*.

> ✳ ***Work It Out:*** *When you think of Jesus, what images come to mind? Are you attracted to Him with awe and wonder? (Please explain.)*

• **Focus on Christ's image.** His beauty comes from the inside out. His eyes radiate with unlimited peace; His smile speaks of incomprehensible joy. Most of all, His heart beats with boundless love.

---

7. Author and missionary Manfred Koehler contributed to today's devotional entry.

✳ **Work It Out:** *Do the negative opinions of skeptics sometimes shake your faith? (Please explain.) Are you able to stick with what God says is right. . .even in the face of doubters?*

• **Pray: "Lord, guide me today; help me know the purpose You have created just for me."** Ask Jesus to give the kind of obedience that Mary demonstrated. Ask Him to focus your vision on His boundless love.

→ NOTES FOR GROWTH

A Key Point I Learned Today:

_____

_____

_____

How I Want to Grow:

_____

_____

_____

My Prayer List:

_____

_____

_____

DAY 4:

GROWING UP GOD

**After three days they found him in the temple courts,
sitting among the teachers, listening to them and
asking them questions. Everyone who heard him was
amazed at his understanding and his answers.**
— Luke 2:46–47

→ SEE HIM

Boy Jesus in the Temple

For young men in Jewish culture, a boy's twelfth birthday marks his passage into manhood and the beginning of some important new stuff to think about: establishing his identity, mission, and beliefs.

Jesus is twelve, nearly thirteen, when His parents take Him to Jerusalem for the Feast of the Passover. Reaching Jerusalem from Nazareth requires a four-day trek over harsh terrain where thieves and outlaws lurk, so many people from their town travel as a group.

When they arrive, Jerusalem is bursting with noisy celebration. Each day, hundreds of people stream in one temple gate with their sheep, while hundreds more stream out another—carrying bloody cuts of meat and the hide of the carcass of the animal they have sacrificed.

As the weeklong feast comes to a close, Mary and Joseph begin their grueling trip home. As Mary walks with the other women, she probably figures Jesus is with Joseph—while Joseph figures He's with her. It's quite a shock when they get together in the evening and discover He isn't with either of them.

Mary and Joseph first comb the camp and then spend three days searching the streets of Jerusalem. They hit all the festival attractions that should interest a boy of Jesus' age, never imagining that He'd be hanging out with religious scholars in the temple. But there He is, politely listening and asking questions of the top teachers—amazing all of them with His solid insights and answers.

Like any mom, Mary is upset when she finally lays eyes on her son. Here's how author Walter Wangerin Jr. re-creates the scene:

Mary flew around the pillars and found some 10 men sitting in a circle, old men, young men—and a boy! Rabbis, they were. Teachers and students and—

"Yeshi!" she shrieked. All talking came to a halt. "Yeshi, what are you doing here?"

Everyone turned and looked at her. Jesus turned, too, but with level eyes and a maddening calm.

A rabbi said, "The lad is studying the Law. He has a marvelous understanding—"

Mary hardly heard him. She ran to Jesus and took His face between her hands. "What have you done to us?" she hissed. She was going to cry. Therefore, she shouted at the top of her lungs: "Your father and I have been searching the city for days! I would never have treated my parents like this! Yeshi, I've been dying with worry!"

"Mama," the boy said, "why did you have to search?"

"What? What are you saying?"

"But didn't you know where I would be? Didn't you know that I must be in my Father's house?"

Mary stopped shouting. She released her son's face, seeing pink marks where her hands had squeezed Him. No, she did not understand this thing which He said. Neither did she understand Him.[1]

1. Wangerin, 613.

Explore the Word: Luke 2:41–52

" 'Why were you searching for me?' he asked. 'Didn't you know I had to be in my Father's house?'" (Luke 2:49). These are the earliest words of Jesus quoted in the New Testament. Before this time, no one had ever referred to God as "my Father." No one had ever spoken about the Creator in such a personal, intimate way. From these few words, we discover a huge, myth-shattering truth about how our young Messiah thinks: He knew His true identity was in serving God and doing His will.

How does a twelve-year-old already realize so much about His responsibilities? He knows He has a responsibility to His parents—but that His responsibility to do His Father's will comes first. He is not distracted by the fact that He knows His actions will cause His parents to worry. He accepts His place in life—He belongs in His Father's house. His focus is on eternity. Selfish desires and living for the moment aren't even an issue.

Even though He was both fully human and fully God, Jesus was able to know completely who He was early in life. We can't understand it. No one knows how much He had to keep His frail, human side in check to stay committed to His values. But as a young man, Jesus shows He did understand who He was—a son to His parents. He returns home with Mary and Joseph, respecting their authority, and the fact that He's God's Son doesn't inflate His ego. He shows humility and still accepts His identity in both heaven and earth.

Even for Jesus, sometimes it was difficult to keep His responsibilities and beliefs straight. He understands our struggles because He went through them, too (remember His temptation in the wilderness?). Although He caused

His parents worry, He never sinned. His journey to manhood was on the right path because His course was set by God.

So don't ever forget to ask yourself: How did Jesus think?

→ KNOW HIM

• **Think differently about yourself.** In the world's eyes, our identity is wrapped up in who we know, what we do, or how we look. But in our heavenly Father's eyes, what matters is whose we are—His. God doesn't value anyone else in the world more than you. He knows you completely—better than you know yourself. And to Him, you are one-of-a-kind, priceless, and loved beyond belief.

> ✳ **Work It Out:** *Does this truth change the way you see yourself? (Why or why not; please explain.) Since human life is precious to God, how should this change the way we see others?*

• **Think about the truth.** Check out these can't-miss insights from J. I. Packer, a Christian scholar who has written several life-changing books: "We were all created to be God's image-bearers.... We are made in such a way, I believe, that we are only at peace with ourselves when it's God's truth that our minds are grasping and consciously obeying. Human life is lacking dignity until you get to that point."[2]

> ✳ **Work It Out:** *Define your values (in three sentences or less). Now connect your definition to J. I. Packer's quote above. Finally, tell why maturity means standing up for what's right and living by your convictions—not what the world says is right.*

---

2. J. I. Packer, *J. I. Packer Answers Questions for Today* (Wheaton, IL: Tyndale House, 2001), 11.

• **Pray: "Lord, help me to think as Jesus thinks and to see myself as You see me."** Ask Jesus to give you courage to seek answers to your questions, the humility to accept them, and the faith to commit your desires fully to Him. Ask Him to bring the sources of His truth into your life that will mold you into the man He wants you to be.

→ NOTES FOR GROWTH

A Key Point I Learned Today:

_____

_____

_____

How I Want to Grow:

_____

_____

_____

My Prayer List:

_____

_____

_____

DAY 5:

JOHN THE BAPTIST PREPARES THE WAY

"I baptize with water," John replied, "but among you stands one you do not know. He is the one who comes after me, the straps of whose sandals I am not worthy to untie."
—John 1:26–27

→ SEE HIM

A Voice Calling in the Desert

A number of the Jews of Jerusalem, the priests, and the Levites don't know what to make of John the Baptist. He lives in the Judean desert, wears rustic camel's hair clothes with a leather belt around his waist, and survives on a diet of locusts and wild honey—much like the descriptions of Elijah.

But in spite of his scary appearance, John can preach . . .and he's drawing big crowds. People gather around him out of spiritual hunger and their fascination with this eccentric personality and commanding voice. And some are starting to whisper among themselves, "Is this the Christ?"

The Savior of Israel has been promised by God for thousands of years, and John even spoke the words of the prophet Isaiah, describing himself as "a voice of one calling: 'In the wilderness, prepare the way for the LORD; make straight in the desert a highway for our God.'"[1]

John is so unusual, the religious leaders know they have to investigate.

---

1. Isaiah 40:3.

"I am not the Christ," John tells them.

Next they ask if he is Elijah, the Old Testament prophet who was whisked up to heaven hundreds of years ago—a man some believed would come back to announce the Christ.

"I am not," John replies.

In desperation they ask for an answer they can take back to their superiors. That's when John quotes Isaiah, essentially telling them, "It's my job to tell you to straighten out your lives because God's on His way!"

Now he's starting to upset the investigators. After all, they came to grill him—not to be preached at. So they demand to know, "Why then do you baptize if you are not the Christ, nor Elijah, nor the Prophet?"

John gives them an answer that they never saw coming. He says that standing right there among them is somebody they don't know—somebody whose sandals he's not even fit to untie. In this culture, untying sandals is considered such a low-level job that only slaves are supposed to do it. So John makes it clear that he's not preaching out of a puffed-up ego or delusions of grandeur. Instead, he's here to prepare everyone for somebody else—somebody he's not even fit to be a slave to.

Suddenly, John has everyone's attention. The "voice of one calling in the desert" is so strong and so persistent that it is heard even in the king's palace.

→ HEAR HIM

Explore the Word: John 1:19–28

There was something about John the Baptist that people took seriously. Wherever he went, people stopped and listened. He seemed to strike a universal chord, one that still rings true today. His words in the book of John pierce hearts with a deep-rooted sense that humanity has failed, that every one of us must find a way to be cleansed of our sins.

The answer: Jesus Christ.

Ordinary folk gravitated to this message, which was simple and practical and filled with hope. The citizens of Israel knew that there was no realistic way for them to ever measure up to the rules of the Pharisees.[2] But when they were baptized in the Jordan River, it was a specific act at a specific time.[3] They knew they were preparing their souls for the arrival of the Messiah.

Biblical scholar Craig G. Bartholomew, PhD, sheds light on some key elements of John's mission as the front-runner of the Lord:

> *John's message is that God's subjects must repent—turn from sin to God, seeking his promised salvation—and be baptized in water. Where this happens is important, since for the Jews geography is drenched with symbolic meaning. John baptizes in the Jordan River because it was here that, more than a thousand years earlier, Israel entered the promised land to become God's light to the nations. John's return to this place signals a new beginning for Israel, a new summons from God to carry out that original (long-neglected) task. Baptism is a vivid symbol of this new beginning, suggesting cleansing from sin. The people of God are (symbolically) crossing the Jordan once more, entering into the land, cleansed and ready to take up their task again.[4]*

2. Anderson, *Jesus*, 30.
3. Ibid.
4. Craig G. Bartholomew and Michael W. Goheen, *The Drama of Scripture: Finding Our Place in the Biblical Story* (Grand Rapids: Baker Academic, 2004), 133.

• **Repent and make way for the Lord.** Are you listening to the "voice of one calling in the desert"? The late English journalist, author, and media personality Malcolm Muggeridge once said this about Jesus Christ: "God reaches down to relate himself to man, and man reaches up to relate himself to God. Time looks into eternity and eternity into time, making now always and always now. Everything is transformed by this sublime drama of the Incarnation, God's special parable for fallen man in a fallen world. . . . By living with, by, and in him, we can be reborn to become new men and women in a new world."[5]

> ✳ ***Work It Out:*** *What does it mean to "make straight the way for the Lord"? How does this command apply to your life?*

• **Let the truth set you free.** "To the Jews who had believed him, Jesus said, 'If you hold to my teaching, you are really my disciples. Then you will know the truth, and the truth will set you free'" (John 8:31–32). In this deceptively simple verse, Jesus tells us that if we follow His teachings, we will learn His truth and be liberated. Sounds great, doesn't it? The problem, though, is that sometimes it looks as if we are following Jesus' teachings pretty well on the outside, but on the inside, we haven't handed over our whole hearts.

> ✳ ***Work It Out:*** *Are you ready to hand over everything—your whole heart—to Jesus? Why or why not? (Please explain.) Share what you need Jesus to cleanse from your life.*

---

5. Malcolm Muggeridge, *The End of Christendom* (Grand Rapids: Eerdmans 1980) 51–54.

• Pray: "Lord, help me understand the wondrous and infinite gift You have given me through the grace of Your Son, Jesus Christ." Ask Him to nudge your heart and to help you to be sensitive to sin, not comfortable with it. Spend some time repenting of your sins.

→ NOTES FOR GROWTH

A Key Point I Learned Today:

_____

_____

_____

How I Want to Grow:

_____

_____

_____

My Prayer List:

_____

_____

_____

DAY 6:

JESUS RECEIVES
THE HOLY SPIRIT

**As Jesus was coming up out of the water, he saw heaven
being torn open and the Spirit descending on him like a
dove. And a voice came from heaven: "You are my Son,
whom I love; with you I am well pleased."**
—Mark 1:10–11

→ See Him

Belief, Baptism. . .and the Boldness of the Holy Spirit

John the Baptist can't believe his own ears. His cousin Jesus
just asked to be baptized by him. And in a moment that
will live forever, Heaven is torn open. Here's how author
Walter Wangerin, Jr., recreates the scene:

> In the midst of the multitudes that come daily to the
> Jordan for baptism, there appears one figure separated
> from the rest. John turns and sees the man standing up-
> river among some reeds, waiting. Reflected sunlight plays
> upward from the water on His face, trilling the flesh below
> his eyebrows and cheekbones, below his nose and his chin.
>
> He has amber eyes, gazing directly at John.
>
> He is clean-shaven, like a Roman—or, it occurs to John,
> like one of the prophets mournful for the future, for they
> would shave their beards.
>
> Amber eyes! John recognizes those golden corneas, pol-
> ished, laconic, and nearly translucent. No one else had such a
> fathomless gaze. This must be the cousin John had not seen

since the Passover when his father had died. Eighteen years ago! This was the One of whom his mother had said once, "He is my Lord."

Jesus begins to wade downriver, to the deeper water where John is standing. "John, baptize Me," the Messiah says.

For a moment John hesitates.

"John," Jesus says, "baptize Me." Without waiting for an assent, He closes His eyes, sinks down, and slips under the water. His long hair lingers on the surface for a short while, then it, too, is pulled down into the darkness and disappears.

Time seems to collapse. John slaps the water with the flat of his hand and cries: "Child of the light and the kingdom to come, rise up!"

There is a continued, shining silence—then Jesus, like a great fish, heaves from the water, and immediately the heavens above them split asunder and there flies down a dove, a white dove, a blindingly white dove that alights on the shoulder of Jesus—white fire beside His face—and in that same instant a voice breaks from heaven, saying, "This is My beloved Son, in whom I am well pleased."

Immediately Jesus begins to move from John toward the eastern shore of the river. His expression is intense but unreadable. His manner seems so nearly wolfish—like a predator following an invisible scent—that the people on land back away and make a path for Him.

Jesus is withdrawing from the public with some fierce purpose.

And then John sees that the white dove is flying in spirals ahead of Jesus, leading the way.

Oh, that is no common dove! That is none other than the Holy Spirit who had brooded over the wild waters of creation and then again over the waters of the flood!

"You, Jesus, greater than me," John whispers, "Your

life shall be more amazing than mine. Whatever the Holy Spirit is driving You now, God help You there! God help You, cousin."[1]

→ HEAR HIM

Explore the Word: Mark 1:9–13

Before launching His ministry, Jesus did three things: He committed His life to fulfilling God's will, no matter the cost; He was publically baptized; He received the Holy Spirit. Jesus knows that the Third Person of the Trinity is the one true "compass" for our souls, the Helper who guides our steps, the very Spirit of Truth.[2]

Part of Christ's baptism was intended to be public—a way to identify with those He came to save; a symbol of solidarity with humanity.[3] But an important part of it was very personal. The Holy Spirit empowered Jesus as He came up out of the water, and then God spoke a blessing into His life: "You are my Son, whom I love; with you I am well pleased."

I (Michael) can only imagine that Jesus kept this memory close to the front of His mind, drawing on its strength as He endured the burden He carried. I, too, hold tight to God's promises as I face a challenge or when I need help figuring out which path to follow. And as I take a step of faith, I remind myself of what God really thinks of me: "This is how God showed his love among us: He sent his one and only Son into the world that we might live through him. This is love: not that we loved God, but that he loved us and sent his Son as an atoning sacrifice for our sins" (1 John 4:9–10).

---

1. Wangerin 620-621
2. See John 14:15–18.
3. Anderson, *Jesus*, 33.

We need God's blessing. We need the Holy Spirit to guide our path.

→ KNOW HIM

• **Ask the Lord to reveal his plan for your life.** As Christ-followers, we must place our will into God's plan rather than attempt to force His will into our plans. Spend time in reflection and prayer this week, asking the Lord to show you His vision for your life. Consider the gifts and talents God has given you. Ask God to reveal what His good, pleasing, and perfect will should look like for you (Romans 12:2).

> ✴ *Work It Out: Are you pursuing God's design*
> *for your life—or are you following your own agenda?*
> *Now ask yourself two fundamental questions:*
> *How do I find my place within the body of Christ?*
> *How do I choose a path in life that will take me in*
> *the direction He desires?*

• **Listen to the Holy Spirit.** When you have a close relationship with Jesus, which is nurtured through prayer and Bible engagement, He will tell you Himself what He wants you to do—moment by moment. Not only does the Lord direct your steps with solid answers from scripture, He also communicates with you throughout the day, answering your questions and offering guidance. You literally walk in His presence minute by minute. The Holy Spirit deals with each believer in a personal and intimate way, convicting, directing, and influencing us. As you grow closer and closer to Jesus, your instincts will become more sensitive to His influence. Your entire mind and spirit will become more in tune to God, and you'll begin to hear Him more clearly, just as you would with any good friend.

✳ **Work It Out:** *The Lord gave you a free will to follow Him—or to disobey. Think about a moment in your life when you sensed the Lord leading you on a specific path in life. Now consider this: The Lord's direction usually comes through your own conscience— a sort of growing conviction that a certain course of action is the one He wants you to take. Or it may be given you in the advice of friends of sound judgment—those you love the most. God speaks sometimes through our circumstances and guides us, closing doors as well as opening them. He will let you know what you must do, and what you must be. What is He saying to you right now?*

• **Pray: "Lord, reveal Your eternal purpose for my life."** Ask Jesus to give you courage to seek answers to your questions, the humility to accept them, and the faith to commit your desires fully to Him. Ask Him to bring the sources of His truth into your life that will mold you into the person He wants you to be.

→ NOTES FOR GROWTH

A Key Point I Learned Today:

_____

_____

_____

How I Want to Grow:

_____

_____

_____

My Prayer List:

_____

_____

_____

DAY 7:

DANGEROUS DESERT TRAINING

Jesus said to him, "Away from me, Satan! For it is written:
'Worship the Lord your God, and serve him only.'
Then the devil left him, and angels came and attended him.
—Matthew 4:10–11

→ SEE HIM

Jesus Overcomes the Devil

Filled with the Holy Spirit, Jesus journeys deep into the wilderness for some intense "spiritual training." The Savior spends forty days and nights trekking through the wastelands of Judea—alone, with no food or shelter. It's a savage, desolate terrain, a dangerous place. At night, the temperatures drop to bone-chilling digits. By midday the heat of the sun grows intolerable.

Weary and fighting the dull ache of starvation, Jesus begins the Test.

Jesus is resting in a shady spot, the shadow of a boulder. His eyes are closed and He's leaning against the giant stone. Suddenly, He senses it—an icy presence, the presence of evil.

The Lord raises His head and squints. A few feet away, a flash of white light rises from the desert into the sky, the radiance of supernatural power. Slowly coming into focus within the center of this light is the image of a handsome man. The light is this curious figure.

With an arrogant yet almost sympathetic tone, the light speaks. "Since You are God's Son, speak the word that will turn these stones into loaves of bread."[1]

At first, Jesus neither stands nor answers. He regards the light as though it were a savage beast sniffing too close to Him. Then He closes His eyes again and in a hoarse voice whispers: "It is written, No one lives by bread alone, but by every word that issues from the mouth of God."

All at once, the cold presence completely engulfs Jesus. A wind arises and begins to howl. When the Lord opens His eyes, He finds that the light has completely surrounded Him, canceling the desert in a pale fog. Then He feels a footing beneath Him. He stands, and the light releases Him, moving to one side, and so Jesus is able to see that He has been transported to the highest corner of the temple wall. Scattered like pebbles below Him is the Holy City, Jerusalem. Here the priests blow trumpets to usher in the New Year. Here the air is thin and the height is giddy.[2]

The icy light speaks again. "Jump, and prove You are the Son of God." The presence goads Him, quoting Psalm 91: "For the Scriptures declare, 'God will send His angels to keep You from harm'—they will prevent You from smashing on the rocks below."[3]

Jesus counters with a citation from Deuteronomy: "It also says not to put the Lord your God to a foolish test!"

In a flash, the Holy City vanishes, and Jesus is no longer on the temple wall. He is now infinitely higher than anything made by human hands. Standing on a cosmic mountain, the presence gestures expansively—pointing out all the earth's kingdoms, how glorious they all are. Then he says, "They're Yours—lock, stock, and barrel. Just fall down on Your knees and worship me, and they're Yours."

But Jesus does not look at the kingdoms of the world, and His refusal is stern: "I know you. I know what sort of angel you are. Satan, tempter, betrayer—get out of here!" The Savior backs His rebuke with another quotation from

---

1. See Matthew 4:3.
2. Wangerin, *Book of Godz*, 623.
3. Ted Miller, *The Story* (Wheaton, Ill.: Tyndale, 1986), 316.

Deuteronomy: "Worship the Lord your God, and only Him. Serve Him with absolute single-heartedness."

In an instant, Jesus is sitting in the desert again, leaning against a boulder. The Test is over and the Devil is gone. In place of the icy presence are warmth and peace and goodness. Angels come down from heaven to care for the Savior.[4]

→ HEAR HIM

Explore the Word: Matthew 4:1–11

When the Deceiver strikes and temptation heats up, Jesus fights back with the perfect offensive weapon: The sword of the Spirit—God's Word (see Hebrews 4:12). It contains truth, and truth can parry or stab the lies of Satan. It has a keen edge that leads to a deadly point. And as the Lord demonstrates, if wielded well, it can attack the enemy and slay temptation before it has a chance to grow into an overpowering monster.

I (Arnie) can attest to the supernatural power in the scriptures. The book of Ephesians lists the things we're to wear when we go into battle against the enemy. Most of the items are defensive. We're given the only offensive weapon we need, "the sword of the Spirit, which is the word of God" (Ephesians 6:17).

Need help resisting the devil? Is temptation getting the best of you? Follow in our Savior's footsteps.

---

4. This story is adapted from Michael Ross, *Tribe: A Warrior's Heart* (Carol Stream, Ill.: Tyndale House Publishers, 2004), 89, 90.

→ Know Him

• **Understand the truth about the enemy.** Satan and his troops are viciously attacking the kingdom of God. His target: our souls. Yet as a created being, Satan is not a sovereign, all-powerful being, and he is certainly not equal to God. What's more, Christianity is not a dualistic religion, a faith in which two opposing but equal powers struggle for control. Even so, many Christ-followers live as though Satan were as powerful as God. Nothing could be further from the truth! Because God is sovereign, Satan does not stand a chance.[5]

✳ *Work It Out: Consider your spiritual weaknesses. Share your biggest temptation right now, as well as what you've found to be most helpful in overcoming it. What temptations and sins hurt your relationship with Jesus?*

• **Take to heart Christ's secrets to winning the battle.** Colossians 3:16 tells Christians to "let the message of Christ dwell among you richly," and Philippians 4:7 promises that "the peace of God. . .will guard your hearts and your minds in Christ Jesus." Hebrews 2:14 assures us that the fear Satan held over humanity was rendered powerless by Christ: "Since the children have flesh and blood, he too shared in their humanity so that by his death he might break the power of him who holds the power of death—that is, the devil."

✳ *Work It Out: The Lord has armed every Christian with spiritual weapons packed with "divine power": (1) the sword of the Spirit—the Holy Bible—and (2) prayer. How will you use these weapons to win the battle over temptation in your life? Is God's Word making a difference in your life? Why or why not? (Explain.)*

---

5. A. Scott Moreau, *Essentials of Spiritual Warfare* (Colorado Springs: Shaw Books, 2000), 111.

• **Pray: "Lord, help me to resist the devil and to turn away from temptation."** Ask Jesus to protect you from Satan's evil schemes. Ask Him to give you victory over sin.

→ NOTES FOR GROWTH

A Key Point I Learned Today:

_____
_____
_____

How I Want to Grow:

_____
_____
_____

My Prayer List:

_____
_____
_____

JESUS IS THE RIGHTEOUS ONE

DAY 8:

FISHERS OF MEN

"Come, follow me," Jesus said, "and I will
send you out to fish for people." At once
they left their nets and followed him.
—Matthew 4:19–20

→ SEE HIM

John—Fisherman and Apostle

Fishing is John's life. He's barely in his late teens, yet he's convinced that throwing nets into the sea and landing the big catch is a good way to make a living. Not only does it put food on his table, but it's also the family thing to do. John and his brother, James, are partners with their father in a prosperous fishing enterprise.

Little does John realize, God has a bigger catch in mind.

One day, while preparing nets as usual with his dad and brother, something amazing happens—an encounter that changes his life forever.

Just off in the distance, not too far away, John spots a man walking along the shore. There's something about His face—a strength matched with gentleness and something like love that makes him unable to look away. When He speaks, His voice is so compelling.

"Follow Me."

That's all He says.

John looks at James with a bewildered expression on his face. James is staring at Him too.

With each footprint the man leaves behind in the

sand, John's heart beats faster. A unique emotion seems to compel him and his brother to leave their nets.

"Who is that?" John asks. But James is already heading toward the unusual man.

→ HEAR HIM

Explore the Word: Matthew 4:18–22

John and his brother chose to follow Jesus, leaving behind much more than just their nets. They abandoned everything that was familiar to them, every earthly pursuit: money, career, popularity, pleasure, the comforts of home. James and John set off on an amazing adventure that became so much more; unwittingly, they had joined a revolution that was going to change history.

For the next few years, the brothers watched as Jesus healed the sick, brought people back from the dead, and spent endless hours reaching out to the lost and the lonely—those whom the world would rather have forgotten. James and John lived with the Savior 24/7, walking hundreds of miles with Him and never once looking back.

If there was anyone who really knew Jesus, these two brothers certainly did. They shared a deep and uncommon connection with the Savior. The Lord brought them into His inner circle, making them His closest friends—even members of the "big twelve" (the original apostles). These guys were on the mountain with Jesus when God the Father dropped by for a little social time (see Luke 9:28–36). And John was the only one whom Jesus asked to look after His mother when He was dying on the cross. What's more, John was the only person to whom Jesus appeared when He described the end times in the book of Revelation.

Talk about connected! And this apostle got right to the point when he wrote his Gospel, starting off with the words: "In the beginning was the Word, and the Word was with God, and the Word was God" (John 1:1).

It's not surprising that his account of Jesus' life is one of the most popular books in the Bible. As we read his writings, we can't help but get the idea that John really loved Jesus. His solid faith literally helped to turn the world upside down (actually, more like right side up). John left behind his old life for something—Someone—much greater.

→ KNOW HIM

• **Break free from your "holy huddle."** Living our lives in a Christian "bubble" makes us feel safe—even comfortable. When our focus is on the huddle, we don't have to deal with scary people on the outside. But here's something interesting to ponder: Our comfort has a very low biblical priority. Jesus doesn't care much about our comfort. If anything, He calls us to spend time *out* of our holy huddle and to impact the world for Him. Throughout the Gospels we see examples of Christ making His disciples uncomfortable by befriending scary people—outcasts. Check out what the Bible says in 2 Corinthians 2:15: "For we are to God the pleasing aroma of Christ among those who are being saved and those who are perishing."

※ *Work It Out: Based on 2 Corinthians 2:15, how do you "smell" to those outside the church?*

• **Tell your story to the world—through words and actions.** Tell others what you're all about, what Christ is all about. Let your actions speak love. Do something that takes you out of your comfort zone and allows you to be a servant to someone. Begin with simple steps: Go next door and tell your neighbor about Jesus—or make Him known to your friends at work, school, or even within your own family. Do some random acts of kindness…such as cleaning a friend's house or volunteering to baby-sit their kids. Invite neighbors to church. Show them that you love them through your actions, not just your words.

> ✴ **Work It Out:** *Think about modern-day outcasts: the handicapped kid who is often overlooked or the loner who doesn't have many friends. Would Jesus visit these people? Would He know their names, care about them, tell them stories? Should you follow Christ's example? (Explain your answer.)*

• **Pray: "God, I know You don't want me to hide my faith; You want me to share it. Please show me how."** Ask Jesus to let His love shine through your life so others will come to Him.

→ NOTES FOR GROWTH

A Key Point I Learned Today:

_____

_____

_____

How I Want to Grow:

_____

_____

_____

My Prayer List:

_____

_____

_____

DAY 9:

RELATIONSHIP, NOT RULES

One Sabbath Jesus was going through the grainfields,
and his disciples began to pick some heads of grain,
rub them in their hands and eat the kernels.
Some of the Pharisees asked, "Why are you doing
what is unlawful on the Sabbath?"
— Luke 6:1–2

→ SEE HIM

Lord of the Sabbath

It's the Sabbath, and Jesus and His followers are picking the heads of grain from open fields and eating them, which isn't stealing. (As if God would do that anyway!)

And as unbelievable as it sounds, Jewish law addresses their actions: "If you enter your neighbor's grain field, you may pick kernels with your hands, but you must not put a sickle to his standing grain."[1]

Yet the Pharisees can't help asking an unnecessary question: "Why are you doing what is unlawful on the Sabbath?"

It's a question the Messiah is hearing quite a bit these days.

Jesus breaks off a head of grain, rubs it in His hands, blows away the chaff, and eats the grain. Then He turns and faces His accusers. But the answer He gives bewilders them.

"Have you never read what David did when he and his companions were hungry?" Jesus asks. "He entered the

---

1. Anderson, *Jesus*, 70.

house of God, and taking the consecrated bread, he ate what is lawful only for priests to eat. And he also gave some to his companions."

The Lord cleverly uses their own scriptures with two examples of similar activity on the Sabbath. And what He says next agitates the Pharisees all the more: "The Son of Man is Lord of the Sabbath." (In other words, I'm in charge—not you.)

Jesus knows that these men are stuck on rules. They just don't understand that He is all about relationships, that He is here to replace the world's oppressive, manmade codes and standards with love—God's perfect, freedom-giving, eternal love.

The Pharisees are too puffed up, too hardheaded, and too deaf to listen. They've invented thousands of additions to God's laws to try to make themselves appear holier. And the truth is, they've been operating this way for so long, they've forgotten what it's like to let God be in charge.

Again and again, Jesus reminds them that God is love—not the Creator of rules!

→ HEAR HIM

Explore the Word: Luke 6:1–11

Does your faith often feel stuck—bogged down by rituals and rules?

Those who are thriving spiritually have clued in to a secret: they know that Christianity is unlike any other world religion. In fact, they understand that it isn't really a religion at all; *it's a relationship*. It's an intimate, minute-by-minute walk with a Person—Jesus Christ. With this distinction driving their hearts and minds, they have found their place within the body. They try to avoid wasting their time on pursuits that counter God's will. They are guided by a clear personal vision of (1) who Christ is, (2) how to connect with Him, and (3) the keys to "putting off" or "putting away" the characteristics of our old life, and "putting on" characteristics of our new life. (See Ephesians 4:22–32.)

Many successful Christ-followers try to zero in on how God wants them to live and what He wants them to accomplish in life. Many have an accurate and precise picture of the work that expresses them best. They have identified their talents and are using them. As a result, these individuals experience profound and lasting benefits: reduced stress, more balance, a more productive career, and a more satisfying life.

→ Know Him

• **Nurture a deeper relationship with Jesus.** How do we get eternal life? Jesus makes that clear, and it sounds deceptively simple, doesn't it? Know God. Know Jesus. The end. But it's not quite that easy. In reality, truly knowing God and Jesus doesn't just happen—faith isn't simply something we declare and move on. Knowing God requires that we nurture a relationship with Him—a relationship that entails two-way communication, listening, sharing, trusting, and growing together. . .just like any earthly relationship we pursue. We all know relationships are work. They require give-and-take, reciprocity, and the same is true for our relationship with God. The beauty, of course, is that even though it's work to pursue a relationship with God, as we begin to see an inner transformation occur as the result, we will be inspired to continue, digging deeper and deeper into relationship with Him.

  ✳ *Work It Out: Name three things that you can do every day that will help you grow closer to Jesus. Are these practical steps—things that you will actually do? When will you get started?*

• **Allow the Lord to realign your priorities.** In the words of author Max Lucado, "One source of man's weariness is the pursuit of things that can never satisfy; but which one of us has not been caught up in that pursuit at some time in our life? Our passions, possessions and pride—these are all *dead* things. When we try to get life out of dead things, the result is only weariness and dissatisfaction."[2] Do you love God with all your heart, mind, and soul? Is knowing Him the passion and priority in your life? Delight in the Lord. Do these things and He will give you the desires of your heart.

> ※ ***Work It Out:*** *When it comes to your faith in Christ, where are your priorities? Is having a deeper, stronger attachment to Jesus your number-one passion, like it was for John? When you blow it, do you admit your mistake, asking your Savior to renew and transform your heart?*

• **Pray: "Lord, help me to leave behind bland rituals and stale religion so I can follow You in a truly living, exciting way."** Don't just read about faith or settle for second-hand knowledge about Jesus. Ask Him for the strength and courage to give up your old life. Ask Him to show you how to *experience* Him daily.

---

2. Max Lucado, *Walking with the Savior* (Wheaton: Tyndale House, 1993), 272.

→ NOTES FOR GROWTH

A Key Point I Learned Today:

_____

_____

_____

How I Want to Grow:

_____

_____

_____

My Prayer List:

_____

_____

_____

DAY 10:

JESUS CLEANS US UP

A man with leprosy came to him and begged him on
his knees, "If you are willing, you can make me clean."
Filled with compassion, Jesus reached out his hand and
touched the man. "I am willing," he said. "Be clean!"
Immediately the leprosy left him and he was cured.
—Mark 1:40–42

→ SEE HIM

Jesus Heals a Leper

Broken. Lonely. Desperate. The outcast spends his life on
the fringes, and his days are lived in the shadows. But news
travels quickly throughout Galilee—even on these forgotten back roads.

The man knows he doesn't have a minute to waste. This
is his only hope. He must reach the center of town. Not
making it there means inevitable destruction. The eternal
end to an already pitiful life.

The man covers his hideous physique in his pungent-
smelling wrap and steps out of a dark alley. Suddenly, a
scream pierces the air. The man peeks out from behind his
hood and watches as a woman grabs her child and races to
the other side of the street.

"Don't come around here!" yells a person on his right.

"Stay away!" screams another. "You know you're not
welcome!"

"Get away from us, unclean one—you LEPER!"

Everywhere he goes, the man is treated like garbage.

But it doesn't stop him. He ignores the biting words and continues to hobble along the hot, dusty road—eventually reaching a crowd at the end of the street.

Standing among the people is the only Man who won't reject him; the one Man who has the power to make him well. A Nazarene. A carpenter. God in the flesh, speaking to the broken and lonely, the desperate and diseased.

And when he reaches Jesus, the most incredible thing happens. The leper falls on his knees and begs, "If You are willing, You can make me clean."

Seeing the man's faith, Jesus is filled with compassion and reaches out His hand to touch the man. "I am willing," He says. "Be clean!"

Immediately the man is cured.

→ HEAR HIM

Explore the Word: Mark 1:40–45

Amazing story. To me (Michael), it's one of the Bible's top-ten most awe-inspiring. I know what you're thinking: *But the Bible has way better stories than this! Like Jesus walking on water, or Moses parting the Red Sea. . .or God digging into the earth and creating humans.*

What's so amazing about this one?

Well, the leper wasn't just some no-name person who got a second chance at life. This guy is just like you and me. He had a repulsive, deadly disease—just like the sin that plagues us all. Oh, sure, we may not have festering sores on the outside, but inside, we all have them.

Each of us has a condition that's every bit as bad, if not worse, than leprosy. It's deadly, and it kills both body and soul.

When the Great Physician reached out His hand and said, "I am willing," He was also talking to you and me.

When that pitiful, struggling, dying man made his way to see the Holy One, and said, "You can make me clean," how did Jesus respond?

Was He grossed out? Did He spit on the man and order him to get lost? Did He turn away and gag?

Jesus did what only a Savior would do. He stretched out His hand and healed.

He also stretches out His hand to you and me today. He loves us in spite of our sin. He wants to forgive us and cure us of our deadly disease—the disease of sin.

"I am willing," He says. "Are you?"

→ KNOW HIM

• **We are healed and made right through Jesus Christ.** Romans 5:18–19 reads, "Consequently, just as one trespass resulted in condemnation for all people, so also one righteous act resulted in justification and life for all people. For just as through the disobedience of the one man the many were made sinners, so also through the obedience of the one man the many will be made righteous." The beauty in this message is that Jesus redeems us, every single one of us, whether we deserve it or not. That's grace, isn't it? An undeserved gift. The fact is, one sin may have condemned us all, but a single act of righteousness—Jesus' death on the cross—saves every one of us and redeems every single one of our sins. God forgives the fact that we sin over and over and over. God overlooks the fact we don't deserve such grace.

✳ *Work It Out: Whenever you've given in to temptation and sin, have you taken action and repented? (Please explain your answer.)*

• **In order to be forgiven, we have to let the forgiver in.** Asking someone for forgiveness requires that we open ourselves up entirely—just as the leper did—not only admitting our wrongdoing but also admitting our vulnerability, fear, and insecurities. . .our innermost self, including all of our hang-ups, neuroses, and sins. Jesus knows how difficult this is. He knows that when we truly ask for forgiveness we are opening ourselves up to a place of vulnerability and risk.

> ✳ *Work It Out: Are you humble enough to recognize the depth of your sin? Are you ready to accept the complete forgiveness God offers? Share what you need Jesus to cleanse from your life.*

• **Pray: "Lord Jesus, 'I am willing' to be healed—and I'm reaching out to You right now."** Ask Jesus to take your hand and to cleanse you.

→ NOTES FOR GROWTH

A Key Point I Learned Today:

_____

_____

_____

How I Want to Grow:

_____

_____

_____

My Prayer List:

_____

_____

_____

DAY 11:

MIRACLE MESSIAH

**Some men came, bringing to him a paralyzed man,
carried by four of them. Since they could not get him
to Jesus because of the crowd, they made an opening
in the roof above Jesus by digging through it and then
lowered the mat the man was lying on. When Jesus
saw their faith, he said to the paralyzed man,
"Son, your sins are forgiven."**
—Mark 2:3–5

→ SEE HIM

Jesus Heals a Paralyzed Man

"Who is this man?"

"The real question is, who does He think He is?"

The teachers of the Law had heard that Jesus was in town, stirring up the crowds with His radical ideas. A few of the skeptical religious leaders had to hear it for themselves—so they made their way into a crowded building and listened with disgust.

The young Jew before them claims to be the Messiah. He even insists that He has all authority on earth, yet He wanders the land like a drifter. What's more, He's a mere carpenter's son and hangs out with society's undesirables: lepers, beggars, prostitutes, traitors.

Suddenly. . .CREAK! SNAP! Wood breaks, clay falls, dust rises.

The Pharisees glare and look up.

A paralyzed man is lowered from the roof and gently placed at Christ's feet.

"Friend," Jesus says, "your sins are forgiven."

What did that man just say? wonders a teacher of the Law. *He's blaspheming! Who can forgive sins but God alone?*

Jesus looks at the Pharisee. "Why are you thinking these things?" He asks. "But that you may know that the Son of Man has authority on earth to forgive sins—"

Jesus turns to the crippled man. "I tell you, get up, take your mat, and go home."

A miracle! The crowd gasps as the formerly paralyzed man stands up and walks out the door. Everyone in the room rejoices. The teachers of the Law stare in shock.

→ Hear Him

Explore the Word: Mark 2:1–12

Jesus knew what His skeptics were thinking and how they were going to react to His miracles, His teachings. . .His mission on earth.

Likewise, God knows our darkest thoughts, anxieties, and fears; He sees what we try to keep hidden from the rest of the world, the worst parts of ourselves.

But we shouldn't feel ashamed or burdened by this, because God always loves us, no matter what; He won't ever abandon us, no matter what lies festering in our darkness. The thing is, God wants access to those dark places; He wants us to let Him in. He wants us to trust Him enough to reveal our truest selves to Him. God takes those dark and ugly parts, shines His light on them, and transforms everything into good.

→ Know Him

• **Don't be ashamed of your flaws.** We are cracked—flawed, broken sinners. But it is in those cracks, in our darkest, most desperate places, that God's light shines the brightest.

It's our choice: Do we seal up those cracks and pretend they aren't there? Or acknowledge our weakness and invite God in to mend our fractures?

※ *Work It Out: What do you need Jesus to heal in your life?*

• **He sacrificed His life for you.** Christ had to be without sin to qualify as the perfect Sacrifice for the sin of mankind—the perfect Sacrifice for your sin. As God's sinless Sacrifice, Jesus made it possible for you to trust in Him and be forgiven.

※ *Work It Out: Does He have your attention? Do you know Him?*

• **Pray: "Lord, help me to know You better."** Ask Jesus to help you give up your own will for the will of God. Ask Him to enable you to daily live a life of spiritual sacrifice for the glory of Christ.

→ NOTES FOR GROWTH

A Key Point I Learned Today:

_____

_____

_____

How I Want to Grow:

_____

_____

_____

My Prayer List:

_____

_____

_____

DAY 12:

MATTHEW MEETS HIS MAKER

**Once again Jesus went out beside the lake. A large
crowd came to him, and he began to teach them. As he
walked along, he saw Levi son of Alphaeus sitting at the
tax collector's booth. "Follow me," Jesus told him,
and Levi got up and followed him.**
— Mark 2:13–14

→ See Him

The Calling of Matthew

Sitting in an open-air booth is very draining during the
summer months for Matthew—a.k.a. Levi. But enduring
the intense heat isn't the half of it. Putting up with the
sarcastic (and even cruel) comments of his fellow citizens
is even more stifling.

Yes, Matthew is Jewish, but he works for the Roman
government. His job requires him to collect taxes from other
Jews in order to fund Caesar's rather elaborate lifestyle. (If
you think governments today take more than their share,
you wouldn't believe what Rome required the citizens of
Israel to cough up.) It's no wonder the Jews hate people like
Matthew. He is considered a traitor. But since he is a Jew,
he is hated by his Roman employers, too.

"Hey, Mr. Tax Man!" Jesus probably probed. "What's
your name?"

At first Matthew ignored the question. Nobody ever
asked him a question expecting an answer. Except maybe
one like, "Do you know how much people hate you?"

"Matthew, my name is Matthew," the wealthy untouchable replied.

Jesus knew what his name in Hebrew meant. "Gift of the Lord." What a joke. The name his mother gave him as a baby wasn't anything close to how he felt about himself. He wasn't a gift of the Lord. As far as his Jewish associates felt, he was a jerk. Perhaps Matthew was rolling in the bucks, but he was lonely as could be. He struggled with guilt. And for good reason. He'd gouged people every day of his life for as long as he could remember in order to feather his comfortable nest.

But Jesus wasn't going to let Matthew off the hook that easily. He was convinced that this spiritually poor rich man could reach a point in his life where he would really see his life as a gift.

"Matthew?" the carpenter-turned-rabbi asked. "Come with Me. Leave your table of injustice and let Me teach you a new career."

Matthew must have been ready for that kind of invitation. It's obvious he wasn't happy with his life. Even without asking what Jesus had in mind, Matthew dropped the canvas flap on his tentlike booth, closed up shop, and made tracks in the hot sand to catch up with the Teacher. He didn't even take the velvet bags of coins that were left piled under his table.

Whatever Jesus saw in Matthew, his invitation to join the other disciples was something Matthew found irresistible. The well-dressed tax man in the expensive threads and manicured beard left his livelihood behind. He started hanging with fishermen whose robes smelled like trout.[1]

→ HEAR HIM

Explore the Word: Mark 2:13–17

In addition to being hated, Matthew was also pretty well off. Scratch that. He was quite well off. In fact, the guy was rich. Many years earlier he'd made peace with the fact that

1. This story is adapted from Jeremy V. Jones, Greg Asimakoupoulos, and Michael Ross, *Tribe: A Warrior's Calling* (Colorado Springs: Focus on the Family, 2006), 24–26.

he wasn't going to have friends (except other tax collectors), so he decided he'd have a comfortable life.

Based on what the Bible tells us, Matthew's base of operation was near the Sea of Galilee. It's likely it was right on the main highway that connected Persia with Egypt. That's where he was when Jesus encountered him. And before the week was out, Matthew planned a party for his friends. You guessed it. They were tax collectors just like him. He spread the word. "YOU'RE INVITED! Bring anyone you can think of. My new friend Jesus is going to be there. I want you to meet Him."

Of course, Jesus showed up. When Jesus approached Matthew at his place of employment, He was genuinely interested in a tax-taker who had no sense of significance in his life. The Nazarene rabbi had His heat sensors on anyone who was hungry for a fresh start at life.

So when Matthew offered to show his guest of honor his well-appointed pad, Jesus most willingly took the VIP tour. He didn't put Matthew down for having such an over-the-top mansion, but He didn't ooh and aah over it either. Matthew could tell that Jesus was more interested in him than in his home.

And Jesus wasn't the only one who showed up. Matthew's down-and-dirty buddies were there, too. They wanted to meet the man responsible for causing Matthew to give up his lucrative occupation. Even though Matthew's profession wasn't the most respectable way to make a living, it provided him with a circle of friends he was able to introduce to Jesus.

In other words, Matthew's past experience was part of what he brought to the table. His friendships, his personality, his confidence in working with money, his ability to mingle with the public, all these aspects of the former tax collector's life were abilities he was now able to use to introduce people to Jesus. In fact, as Matthew grew in his faith, he wrote the first book of the New Testament. It's the one that bears his name. It also bears witness to all Matthew had seen and heard growing up in a Jewish community. Of the four accounts of Jesus' life and ministry, Matthew's Gospel explains the good news of God's love in a way that Jewish people could understand.

Isn't that fascinating? Not only does God call people to be part of His plan to change the world; He makes use of what they have to offer. You could probably even make a case for believing that the bents and abilities we are born with were given to us in anticipation of the day we would accept Jesus and start serving Him.

→ KNOW HIM

• **Ponder how you became a disciple of Jesus.** Your testimony may not be as dramatic as some you've heard. But it's your story. Go ahead, pull out your journal and write it down. Describe what was going on in your life before you decided to take Jesus seriously. Then make note of who influenced you spiritually and why you were open to what they shared. Finally, take note of how Jesus has impacted your life since. You never know who might want to hear how God has been active in your life.

> ✳ *Work It Out: Verbalize what you've written. How did you come to Christ? (Please share your testimony.)*

• **Know that God has given each one of us a unique place to serve.** 1 Corinthians 12:12 reads, "Juast as a body, though one, has many parts, but all its parts form one body, so it is with Christ." We are not just a bunch of random humans who have been thrown into this world to bump around and fumble our way through life. We, each and every one of us, have been designed in the image of God. We all have a purpose and we fit together by His great design.

✳ *Work It Out:* *When the Lord gives you an assignment, do you accept it with a trusting heart,
or do you shrink back and tell Him that you are
unqualified for the job? How does it make you feel,
knowing that those in Christ's inner circle were
rough around the edges?*

• **Pray: "Lord, help me understand what it means to belong to you."** Thank Jesus that He called you to be part of
His team to reach the world. Ask Him for courage to keep
from caving in to what others think is important.

→ NOTES FOR GROWTH

A Key Point I Learned Today:

_____

_____

_____

How I Want to Grow:

_____

_____

_____

My Prayer List:

_____

_____

_____

DAY 13:

TEAM JESUS AND
THE JOURNEY

**When morning came, he called his disciples to him
and chose twelve of them, whom he also designated
apostles: Simon (whom he named Peter), his brother
Andrew, James, John, Philip, Bartholomew, Matthew,
Thomas, James son of Alphaeus, Simon who was called
the Zealot, Judas son of James, and Judas Iscariot,
who became a traitor.**
— Luke 6:13-16

→ SEE HIM

Ordinary Men on an Extraordinary Mission

After fending off the Pharisees' accusations that Jesus
doesn't honor the Sabbath, the Savior turns His thoughts
to more important matters: Who will be His apostles?
Who will be His inner circle of close friends? Jesus spends
the entire night praying to the heavenly Father, and then
He chooses the Twelve—ordinary men with different
backgrounds. None was theologically trained or part of the
official religious leadership in Israel. In Jesus' eyes, this is
the perfect mix and the right choice to spread the Gospel
after He leaves.

Matthew, the tax collector, is considered a traitor to his
country, while Simon the Zealot belongs to an organiza-
tion that wants to kill all traitors. The twelve men make an
interesting combination, but the love of Jesus breaks down

all barriers and teaches them to work with one another and to love one another.

Jesus now begins His famous Sermon on the Mount, considered by many scholars to be history's greatest teaching.

Our Savior starts off by saying how blessed we are if we're poor, hungry, weeping, and even hated because of Him. In fact, He says if we are insulted because of Him, "rejoice in that day and leap for joy, because great is [our] reward in heaven" (Luke 6:23). In other words, if we're really letting Jesus be Lord, our rewards won't always come through outward situations. But we can have the peace, the love, and the joy of the Holy Spirit bubbling up and overflowing inside us, something that no amount of money can buy. All that, plus the eternal rewards in heaven. Kind of a two-for-one deal. Not bad. Not bad at all. In fact, it's terrific!

On the other hand, if we're still chasing after the world, its riches, its superficial happiness, and its fame, we may get what we want—but that's all. There'll be no eternal life and no inner peace. In fact, Jesus says such people will be unhappy. Not only that, but they will miss out on eternity. After their worldly pride and fun wear off, the things they valued will become completely worthless.[1]

→ HEAR HIM

Explore the Word: Luke 6:12–26

When I (Arnie) was a child, I remember how much I wanted something for Christmas. Whatever I got was fun for a while, but as the weeks passed, I got bored and wanted something else. The same is still true, whether the coveted toy is a new computer, an expensive sports car, or diamonds and pearls.

Nothing can possibly fill that empty space in our hearts that was especially designed for God to fill—except God Himself.

---

1. A portion of this story was adapted from Bill Myers and Michael Ross, *Faith Encounter: Experience the Ultimate With Jesus* (Eugene: Harvest House Publishers, 1999), 74-75.

So in the days ahead. . .

Cling to the truth. When the going gets rough in life and we feel the temptation of breaking away from Jesus and operating on our own strength, remember this truth: *God loves you and knows what He's doing.*

Stay on course. If we've made the decision to follow God, rest assured that the trip will be incredible (if it hasn't been already). We'll go places we've never dreamed about; we'll see things we never imagined. Granted, we will go through rain, blizzards, and storms of various kinds, but as long as we stay under His protection, we'll make it. The storm will pass, life will get better, and we'll find complete fulfillment.

→ Know Him

• **Live by faith**. So much of what we "know" about the world around us is based on what we see with our own eyes. Yet what happens when we see things we can't control, circumstances we can't fix? What happens when our loved one is dying before our very eyes and we can do nothing to help? Or when we witness abuse, poverty, sickness, violence, hunger, or homelessness and are powerless to end it on our own? It's then that we must live by faith, in confident trust that God is gracious, merciful, and loving and knowing that He has the power to transform all circumstances into good. We must hand over everything—our lives, ourselves, our circumstances—to Him.

> ✳ *Work It Out: Do you need to let go of your tight grip on circumstances in your life—or even a relationship? (Please explain.) What steps can you take to hand over control and surrender everything to Jesus?*

• **Remember that we are created specifically and intentionally by our Creator.** Matthew 10:30–31 reads, "And even the very hairs of your head are numbered. So don't be afraid; you are worth more than many sparrows." Throughout the history of mankind, there will never be another "me." I'm unique, you're unique, each and every person who has ever lived is unique! On purpose. We have things in common, like we all have a body. We all need to breathe, eat, and sleep. We all have a hunger to know God and want to live with a purpose. But we each do so in our own unique way—because that is how we have been created.

＊ *Work It Out: How does it make you feel, considering that God knows you inside-out?*

• **Pray: "Lord, help me to find satisfaction in You—not from the world."** Ask Him to help you live by faith.

→ NOTES FOR GROWTH

A Key Point I Learned Today:

_____

_____

_____

How I Want to Grow:

_____

_____

_____

My Prayer List:

_____

_____

_____

DAY 14:

MESSAGE ON THE MOUNT

**Now when Jesus saw the crowds, he went up on
a mountainside and sat down. His disciples
came to him, and he began to teach them.
— Matthew 5:1–2**

→ SEE HIM

Jesus Teaches on the Mountain

In the Sermon on the Mount, Jesus is speaking of love—
not the gushy sentimentality that we often see on TV. He's
talking about His definition of love. And the crowds are
listening.

As Jesus uses the word *love* He often refers to action—
something we *do* rather than something we *feel*. "God so
loved the world that he gave. . ."[1]

He talks to the crowds about love as an action; something that God did for us. And at other moments during
His sermon, He defines love as selfless giving to others, as
manifesting attitudes of kindness, patience, humility, and
commitment in relationships.

→ HEAR HIM

Explore the Word: Matthew 5:1–12

More than two thousand years after Jesus preached the
Sermon on the Mount, His words still echo in our ears
with power, and His teachings continue to surpass all human teachings. Here's how Dr. Henrietta C. Mears once

1. John 3:16.

described Christ's transformational message:

> *Many a person who is not a Christian claims that the Sermon on the Mount is his or her religion. How little this person understands the depth of that sermon's meaning! It is important that we don't simply praise what Jesus said as a wonderful theory but that we actually practice it in our own lives. If we let this rule operate in our lives, it will change our personal relations, heal our social wounds and solve every dispute between nations— yes, it will set the whole world in order.*[2]

Jesus was a master teacher, and His words were unlike anything the crowds had ever heard. As the masses sat at His feet, they hoped to hear the plans of a political leader. Jesus gave them so much more: lessons about how God's people are supposed to live—not by laws, but by love. Jesus shared eight beatitudes, qualities His followers must grow and nurture in their lives.

→ KNOW HIM

• **Grow deeper by *experiencing* Him daily.** Learning about the Lord from a theology textbook is much different from experiencing Him personally in a day-to-day walk. According to the apostle Paul, it's all about faith and fellowship: "I consider everything a loss because of the surpassing worth of knowing Christ Jesus my Lord, for whose sake I have lost all things. I consider them garbage, that I may gain Christ and be found in him, not having a righteousness of my own that comes from the law, but that which is through faith in Christ—the righteousness that comes from God on the basis of faith" (Philippians 3:8–9).

---

2. Henrietta C. Mears, *What Jesus Is All About* (Ventura, Calif.: Regal 2004), 43

*✳ **Work It Out:** Of the beatitudes Jesus shares, which ones do you want to develop in your life? How would you describe Christ's light in your life—a flickering candle, a crackling campfire, or a blazing furnace? What can you do to stoke the fire?*

• **Know the keys to following Jesus.** "To the Jews who had believed him, Jesus said, 'If you hold to my teaching, you are really my disciples. Then you will know the truth, and the truth will set you free' " (John 8:31–32). In this deceptively simple verse, Jesus tells us that if we follow His teachings, we will learn His truth and be liberated. Sounds great, doesn't it? The problem, though, is that sometimes it looks like we are following Jesus' teachings pretty well on the outside, but on the inside, we haven't handed over our whole hearts.

*✳ **Work It Out:** Of Christ's teachings, which ones are the hardest for you to follow?*

• **Pray:** "Lord, help me identify the barriers I've erected that keep me from loving You with my whole heart." Ask Jesus to help you trust Him so that you can be freed.

→ NOTES FOR GROWTH

A Key Point I Learned Today:

_____

_____

_____

How I Want to Grow:

_____

_____

_____

My Prayer List:

_____

_____

_____

JESUS IS THE
TRUE HIGH PRIEST

DAY 15:

THE NARROW ROAD TO HEAVEN

"Enter through the narrow gate. For wide is the gate and broad is the road that leads to destruction, and many enter through it. But small is the gate and narrow the road that leads to life, and only a few find it."
— Matthew 7:13-14

→ SEE HIM

The Way of the Wise

Emotions are heating up as Jesus speaks. His Sermon on the Mount teaches the values of His kingdom, and these are puzzling the Jewish people.

"No one can serve two masters," He says. "Either you will hate the one and love the other, or you will be devoted to the one and despise the other. You cannot serve both God and money."[1]

Essentially, Christ is telling the crowds that wealth, the law, and the values of this world that people hold so high can't get them into the kingdom. In fact, relying only on these things "is the road that leads to destruction."

Just about everything He is teaching points in a direction that most people aren't willing to go. His commands don't just forbid murder and adultery; Jesus says they include even hatred and lust (the inner attitudes behind the actions).

And then He hits the crowd right between the eyes: "Not everyone who says to me, 'Lord, Lord,' will enter the kingdom of heaven, but only the one who does the will of my Father who is in heaven."[2]

---

1. Matthew 6:24
2. A portion of this story was adapted from Bill Myers and Michael Ross, *Faith Encounter: Experience the Ultimate With Jesus* (Eugene, Oregon: Harvest House Publishers, 1999), 86-87.

→ HEAR HIM

Explore the Word: Matthew 7:13–23

Is Jesus holding up a standard that is too high for anyone to attain? Not at all. His point is this: It's not about good behavior and human ability. It's about a minute-by-minute relationship with Him. Jesus is the One who empowers us to follow His path. He's the One who gives us the power not to sin. And if we mess up, He'll *always* forgive us and help us start over again.

For most of us, heaven is a lifetime away, so we're tempted to look to the easy route. Many people point us toward this easy, wide road: friends at work and at school, much of the media, political leaders. Unfortunately, the easy route doesn't head in the right direction.

But other people point us toward the right road—the narrow one: pastors, family members, our brothers and sisters in Christ, and, of course, Jesus Himself.

Which kingdom will we finally reach? God has made it clear which one He wants us to choose. Now it's our turn to make the choice.

Confess. Are there sins we need to talk to Jesus about? Coming clean is crucial to building a deeper relationship with Him.

Submit. If Jesus Christ is truly our Lord, that means He's our Master. We must make an effort to obey Him and to rely on His strength (Psalm 28:7).

Dedicate. Knowing God is a lifelong process. We must commit to spending time with Him every day—making our relationship with Him our top priority.

→ KNOW HIM

• **Choose the narrow way.** We must be willing to give up everything—ourselves, our possessions, our pride, our power—in order to gain what God has in store for us. It's sometimes true that in doing so we may never achieve what we dreamed we'd always become. However, when a person fully surrenders his or her life, God often returns those dreams and talents. But one thing is always true: God's plans for us are bigger, grander, and far better than we could ever imagine.

> ✳ *Work It Out: Do you tend to walk more on the broad road or the narrow one? (Be honest and explain your answer.) What makes the narrow gate so hard to find?*

• **Live God's Word.** It's easy to close the Bible after our morning quiet time or at night before we turn off the bedside lamp and feel good about ourselves. "Hey," we rationalize, "I'm reading the Bible, right? Isn't that good enough?" Reading the Bible is a great start, for sure. But God wants us to take another step: He wants us, to live His Word: to ponder it, meditate on it, carry it with us, and act on it. He wants His Word to guide our everyday decisions, serving as a lamp that shines along our daily path and a sounding board against which we can weigh our choices. God's Word *can* indeed seep into our body and spirit, into our heart, mind, and soul. It's our choice: Will we allow God's Word to transform us?

> ✳ *Work It Out: Tell how engaging the Bible can help us find the narrow way.*

• **Pray: "Lord, help me to never put my own desires before You."** Ask Him to put in you a desire for the narrow way—not what's easy.

→ NOTES FOR GROWTH

A Key Point I Learned Today:

_____

_____

_____

How I Want to Grow:

_____

_____

_____

My Prayer List:

_____

_____

_____

DAY 16:

FIVE THOUSAND
MOUTHS TO FEED

**Jesus then took the loaves, gave thanks,
and distributed to those who were seated as much
as they wanted. He did the same with the fish.**
— John 6:11

→ SEE HIM

A Little Faith Goes a Long Way

Everyone is hungry, it's late in the afternoon, and Jesus and
His followers are on the outskirts of nowhere.

The twelve disciples, though tired, do some investiga-
tion on their own while Jesus is dealing with the people.
They calculate the crowd to total around five thousand
men, plus women and children—and they know it can turn
into an unhappy mob when dinnertime and darkness arrive. Besides, they are hungry themselves and they want to
get Jesus alone to report on what they had done to fulfill
His earlier orders.

It must seem obvious to them that Jesus is so caught
up in the people and their individual problems that He is
unaware of the growing difficulty facing them as the sun
goes down in the west. As a group, they push through the
crowd and interrupt Jesus. "This is an out-of-the-way place,
and it's getting really late. Send these people away so they
can spread out to area villages and buy themselves something to eat."

Jesus looks at His disciples and replies, "You give them
something to eat."

He seems to be looking right at Philip, who is from that side of the lake, maybe implying that Philip should know where to find food.

Feeling defensive, Philip does not want to take responsibility for them. He tells Jesus, "Even if we had eight months' wages, it wouldn't be enough money to buy one bite of bread per mouth!" It simply is far too expensive.

Andrew is watching and listening, trying to figure out how he can help. By Philip's calculations, it can't be done. Andrew tries to find a way. His suggestion doesn't seem to have much potential, but he tells Jesus, his voice tentative, "I found a boy with five little barley loaves and a couple of small fish, but that's not going to feed all these people." It isn't much, but the child is willing to share what he has. (Those close enough to hear must be smiling and wanting to laugh.) The boy's resources are cute but pointless!

Jesus doesn't laugh. Instead, He says, "Bring the boy's lunch here to Me," and he tells His disciples to seat the crowd in small groups on the grass.

No doubt the Twelve are at least bewildered if not annoyed. The crowd slowly hushes and sorts itself into groups of fifty to a hundred each. It is surprisingly quiet, and Jesus' voice carries well. He holds the five loaves and two fish in His hands, looks upward, and prays a prayer of gratitude. The loaves are small, about the length of Jesus' hand. He breaks each one of them in pieces and does the same with each of the fish. Then He gives the pieces to His twelve disciples and tells them to start handing them out to the people.

What begins with skepticism grows into awe and satisfaction.

No matter how much the Twelve dole out, there is always more. The impromptu supper guests eat until everyone is full and don't want any more. Jesus tells them, "Gather the leftovers. Don't waste any food."

At the end of the day, a dozen baskets are full to overflowing with pieces of bread and fish.[1]

---

1. Adapted from Anderson, *Jesus*, 124–26.

Explore the Word: John 6:1–15

The twelve disciples are bone weary from their travels—weeks of teaching and healing the multitudes. And now Jesus wants them to feed the crowds? Impossible! Yet a boy offers all he has: five little barley loaves and a couple of small fish. That is more than enough for Jesus to do the miraculous. And what began as skepticism grows into awe and satisfaction.

Previous miracles had been personal. This miraculous meal was for everyone. The hushed awe quickly shifted into shared adrenaline. With exuberant praise for Jesus, some began to say, "This Jesus has to be the Prophet of God." He was a new Moses—like the original Moses who miraculously fed the people of Israel with manna, bread that God sent from the sky every day. Only the God-sent Messiah could have done this. "He should be king!" enthusiastic voices cried.

Jesus wasn't responding to their political enthusiasm, and the mood started to shift. They were going to make Him king by acclamation. Force Him to the throne. After all, anyone who could feed a crowd of thousands with a boy's lunch could recruit, mobilize, and feed an army stronger than the Romans. They had been waiting for this opportunity for half a millennium, and they weren't going to let Jesus decline.

Immediately Jesus gathered His twelve disciples and hurried them into the boat with orders for them to leave Him and row to Bethsaida on the western slope of Galilee Lake near Capernaum. Jesus dismissed the crowd and—with an escape that itself bordered on miraculous—slipped away from the people and climbed up alone on the nearby mountainside to pray.

→ Know Him

• **Know that Jesus is your provider.** Try keeping a simple gratitude list to help you focus on the gifts God lavishes on you every day. Keep your eyes and ears open for the presence of God and then jot these occurrences into a notebook. Sometimes it's helpful to go back to review a concrete record of God's blessings in our lives and take note of the big picture.

> ✳ *Work It Out: Describe a time when Jesus has stretched your limited resources—and turned your skepticism into awe. How has that memory helped your faith grow? What miracles do you need Jesus to perform in your life?*

• **Know that Jesus' miracles are all around us.** It's easy to read today's story and think, *Well, it was easier to see the hand of God at work in Bible times, but what about now? Where are the signs that show the almighty, awesome God in the here and now?* The truth is, though, God shows us His presence every day, through signs and wonders big and small. But in the tumult of our fast-paced days, we don't slow down long enough to glimpse His work. We don't stop long enough to quiet the cacophony of iPods and iPhones, televisions, radios, and the Internet to hear the whispers He intends just for us. Our almighty God is with us—we simply need to open our ears to hear and our eyes to see.

> ✳ *Work It Out: Sometime soon, unplug from all things electronic—especially your cell phone. Grab your Bible and a notebook and spend some time alone with Jesus. Read, pray, and write. Above all, listen. How do you feel as you anticipate doing this? Do you think Jesus will show up and "whisper" something to you? (Why or why not? Please explain.) Share what the two of you may end up talking about.*

• Pray: "Lord, I am always on the go, moving at a frenetic pace with my eyes focused on accomplishing the next thing. Help me slow down so that I can see and hear You." Ask Him to help you experience His awesome presence in your daily life.

→ NOTES FOR GROWTH

A Key Point I Learned Today:

_____

_____

_____

How I Want to Grow:

_____

_____

_____

My Prayer List:

_____

_____

_____

DAY 17:

OUT OF THE COFFIN

Then he went up and touched the the the bier they were carrying him on, and the bearers stood still. He said, "Young man, I say to you, get up!" The dead man sat up and began to talk, and Jesus gave him back to his mother.
— Luke 7:14–15

→ SEE HIM

Jesus Raises a Widow's Son

Jesus pauses on the edge of Nain, a small town about a day's walk from Capernaum, and takes in a heartbreaking sight: a loud but mournful group heading to the local graveyard.

Professional mourners lead the procession, clanging cymbals, playing flutes, and wailing. (It was sort of a custom in that day to hire these guys.) The mother walks alone behind this sad crowd. Men follow behind, carrying the coffin containing her dead son.

A mother losing her only child is a painful thought. What's more, the woman's husband is also dead. This means she's now completely alone. To whom will she turn? How will she survive? Who can possibly comfort her now? Her heartache and misery must be unbearable.

As Jesus' eyes meet hers, He is filled with compassion.

But in this instance, Jesus does more than just feel sad. He stops the procession and exercises His authority over death—and something amazing happens. The boy comes back to life and crawls out of the coffin!

→ Hear Him

Explore the Word: Luke 7:11–17

For me (Arnie) it's comforting to know that as we go through heartache, pain, and suffering, Jesus is right there by our side, feeling every tear, every ache, every bit of sorrow. And Jesus wants you to care about others in the same way. He wants you to see people with "new eyes."

While most Christian guys understand that their lives could—and should—be a reflection of Jesus Christ, they often allow fear of their peers to get in the way. But if God—the One who created us—says we are worthy of His love, why do we pursue what our culture thinks is cool in order to feel good about ourselves?

The key is allowing the Holy Spirit and the truth of the Bible to saturate your heart, mind, and soul. Let the One who created you and everything else in this world reshape your heart, redefine your self-worth—and refocus your vision.

Are you ready for some "eye surgery"? It all begins by following Christ's example.

→ Know Him

• **Ask Jesus to give you eyes to see**—to show you how to be merciful, just as He is merciful. Christ reached out to the unlovable, befriended those whom the world would rather forget, and touched those who seemed untouchable. He sees our value. Compassion is a core Christian quality, and next to Christ Himself, no other person on earth has come to represent the compassion of God more than Mother Teresa. As she has said, "We all long for heaven where God is, but we have it in our power to be in heaven with Him right now—to be happy with Him at this very moment. But being happy with Him now means loving like He loves, helping like He helps, giving as He gives, serving as He serves, rescuing as He rescues, being with Him twenty-four hours a day—touching Him in His distressing disguise."

✳ *Work It Out: Are you willing to show kindness to an outcast? (You know—that family at church that seems a little rough around the edges; that kid at school everybody else picks on.) How will getting to know the outcasts give you "eyes of compassion"?*

• **Trust Christ's power.** If you've ever weathered a period of grief, illness, loss, anxiety, or despair, you probably know what it's like to doubt, to question if God really does have the power to overcome sin and evil and death. Sometimes we are so lost in ourselves, in our own misery and grief, that it's difficult to see and feel God's ever-present goodness and love. We wonder where He is, why He has allowed such circumstances to occur, why He hasn't protected us from such misery. It's perfectly normal to feel this way from time to time, especially during periods of great strife. But throughout those periods, it's important to remember that God's light always overcomes darkness, even when it doesn't feel quite possible.

✳ *Work It Out: How does Jesus' power over death affect the way you live your life? The Lord wants our trust and complete authority over our hearts. Does He have it? Is anything blocking your relationship with Him?*

• **Pray: "Lord, teach me to see others the way You see them."** Ask Jesus to enable you to see a person's worth. Ask Him to help you commit to praying for your friends on a daily basis.

→ NOTES FOR GROWTH

A Key Point I Learned Today:

_____

_____

_____

How I Want to Grow:

_____

_____

_____

My Prayer List:

_____

_____

_____

DAY 18:

JESUS WALKS ON WATER

Shortly before dawn Jesus went out to them, walking on the lake. When the disciples saw him walking on the lake, they were terrified. "It's a ghost," they said, and cried out in fear.

—Matthew 14:25–26

→ SEE HIM

"Step Out of the Boat and Take My Hand!"

The disciples are in trouble. It's about three in the morning and they are crammed in a tiny fishing boat, desperately trying to flee a storm that's pounding the lake. But the rowing is hard and the men are exhausted.

Suddenly, fear turns to terror. Right there atop the waves they spot a human form...*walking* on the water!

Their response? Not exactly a "ten" on the Richter scale of faith.

"It's a ghost!" they shout to one another.

At this point, they should be saying, "Lord, once again we see You are who You claim to be. Thank You for coming to save us!" But instead, they freak.

Jesus hears them and smiles. "Take heart," He says. "Don't be afraid. It's me!"

→ HEAR HIM

Explore the Word: Matthew 14:22–33

Today's passage takes place right after Jesus fed the multitude with the boy's loaves and fish. When the people realize the miracle Jesus performed, they want to make Him king—and they are willing to take Him by force to do so. One of the reasons for this is that for years the Jews have been forced to live under Roman rule. So you can understand why, after seeing all His miracles, the Jews think they can use Jesus to do a little Roman-bashing.

But Jesus will not be manipulated. God wants to give the people overflowing life, but on His terms. He wants to save these people—but He wants to save them from Satan's clutches, not from the Romans. He wants to give them what they really need, not what they want.

So what does Jesus do when they try to force Him to play by their rules? He just sort of. . .disappears.

How often does He do that in our lives? When we try to force God to do something our way, how often does He seem to bow out? But Jesus is never far away.

And then the scene shifts to the disciples and the terrible time they're having on the lake. And what do they—and really all of us—learn? We can trust that Christ is our protector. We can take comfort in this truth the next time we are frightened or confused about something. Jesus isn't there to tell us we're irresponsible for getting caught in a storm. He's not there to yell at us for having so little faith. Instead, He's always there to watch over us, to encourage us, to ease our fears.

He is always there, willing to climb into our boat and weather the storm with us.[1]

→ Know Him

• **Struggle is simply a part of life.** Yet as we encounter a trial, what happens? Fear begins to take over. It seems as if struggle and fear go hand in hand. In fact, fear is one of Satan's favorite tools to use against us. But the good news is,

---

1. A portion of this story was adapted from Bill Myers and Michael Ross, *Faith Encounter: Experience the Ultimate With Jesus* (Eugene Harvest House Publishers, 1999), 104-105.

God tells us—from the beginning of the Bible to the end—that He has conquered fear and has overcome the trials and tribulations of this world. We are no longer slaves to them. As His children we are free! So whenever we struggle and begin to feel paralyzed by fear, here's what we should do: (1) Accept our circumstances, (2) acknowledge fear, and (3) surrender our emotions and our trials to God.

> ✳ ***Work It Out:*** *Have you ever been frightened by Jesus? (Please explain.) If you were in the boat that night, would you have reacted the way Peter did? How are you stepping out of the boat and taking risks? What might keep you in the boat. . .or cause you to sink?*

• **In times of distress call out to Jesus.** He will empower us with the Holy Spirit, and He will help us to handle whatever it is that we must face. Henry T. Blackaby reminds us of the supernatural strength that's available to every believer: "You will never fully understand how God could give you peace in some of the situations you face, but you do not have to understand it in order to experience it. . . .Scripture says to be anxious for nothing. God's Word clearly indicates that there is nothing you can face that is too difficult, too troubling, or too fearful for God."[2]

> ✳ ***Work It Out:*** *When life feels out of control and you fear you're on the verge of "sinking," do you extend a hand to Jesus. . .or do you try to swim on your own? (Explain your answer.)*

• **Pray: "Lord, help me to remember that You are faithful and that You can be trusted."** Ask Jesus to remind you of this every day and to help you pray through difficult circumstances.

---

2. Henry T. Blackaby and Richard Blackaby, *Experiencing God Day-by-Day* (Nashville: Broadman & Holman, 1998), 39.

→ NOTES FOR GROWTH

A Key Point I Learned Today:

_____

_____

_____

How I Want to Grow:

_____

_____

_____

My Prayer List:

_____

_____

_____

DAY 19:

"WHO DO YOU SAY I AM?"

When Jesus came to the region of
Caesarea Philippi, he asked his disciples,
"Who do people say the Son of Man is?"
—Matthew 16:13

→ SEE HIM

"You Are the Christ, the Son of the Living God"

After Jesus arrives in the villages of Caesarea Philippi, He asks His disciples, "What are people saying about who the Son of Man is?"

They reply, "Some think He is John the Baptizer, some say Elijah, some Jeremiah or one of the other prophets."

He presses them, "And how about you? Who do you say I am?"

Simon Peter says, "You're the Christ, the Messiah, the Son of the living God."

Jesus comes back, "God bless you, Simon, son of Jonah! You didn't get that answer out of books or from teachers. My Father in heaven, God Himself, let you in on this secret of who I really am. And now I'm going to tell you who you are, *really* are. You are Peter, a rock. This is the rock on which I will put together my church, a church so expansive with energy that not even the gates of hell will be able to keep it out.

"And that's not all. You will have complete and free access to God's kingdom, keys to open any and every door: no more barriers between heaven and earth, earth and heaven. A yes on earth is a yes in heaven. A no on earth is a no in heaven."

He asks the disciples to remain secret about His identity. He makes them promise they will tell no one that He is the Messiah.

→ HEAR HIM

Explore the Word: Matthew 16:13–28

Jesus became nothing so that we could have everything.

He wore a crown of thorns so that we might wear a crown of glory. He ate with men so we could someday dine with God. He became sin so that we might become righteousness. He cried tears on earth so we would never shed them in heaven. He walked over dusty roads so we could walk on golden streets.

He died so that we might live.

So who was this Man whose life—and death—changed the course of history?

No beauty. Isaiah foretold the agonies of Christ on the cross hundreds of years before Jesus was born. He also knew something about Jesus' appearance: "He had no beauty or majesty to attract us to him, nothing in his appearance that we should desire him" (Isaiah 53:2).

If He had no outward beauty, then why were so many people attracted to Him? Christ's beauty was internal. His heart emanated unlimited love. The peace in His eyes drew crowds. The joy of His smile was contagious. Jesus didn't have good looks—He didn't need them.

No popularity. The Bible also describes Jesus as One who "made himself nothing by taking the very nature of a servant, being made in human likeness" (Philippians 2:7).

Christ was born in an animal shelter in the hick town of Bethlehem and was raised in the boondocks of Galilee by an average-joe carpenter. Later in life, in spite of the many times He helped others, people forgot to thank Him, asked Him to shove off, and tried to make Him look stupid. Those who hung around Him soon left, some of them running. If anything, Jesus had a bad reputation, bad enough to get Himself killed on a cross.

No sin. The Bible stamps the words "no sin" on the person of Christ three times:

"God made him who had no sin to be sin for us, so that in him we might become the righteousness of God" (2 Corinthians 5:21).

"He committed no sin, and no deceit was found in his mouth" (1 Peter 2:22).

"But you know that he appeared so that he might take away our sins. And in him is no sin" (1 John 3:5).[1]

→ KNOW HIM

• **Focus on the God of the Bible.** If you were to peer into a telescope and study the heavens, you would no doubt conclude, as C. S. Lewis remarked, that our Creator is "quite merciless and no friend to man. . . . The universe is dangerous and terrifying." Now consider this picture of God from scripture: a forgiving father embracing his prodigal son. It's important that you know the truth about God. Wrong thoughts about our Lord will cripple your Christian walk, for an idol of the mind is as dangerous as an idol of the hands.[2]

✳ *Work It Out: Have you ever been deceived by mistruths about Jesus? (Please explain.) Make a list of the names the Bible gives to the Lord.*

• **Holiness and love are part of God's essence.** Yet consider this: God's holiness cannot help but destroy every unholy thing that comes into His presence. This truth is difficult to comprehend because, as sinners, we are far from it. On

1. Author and missionary Manfred Koehler contributed to today's devotional entry.

2. *Grow Your Christian Life* (Downers Grove.: InterVarsity Press, 1962), 21.

the flip side, God's love is also something we can't quite grasp. And because of it, He forgives our sin through Jesus Christ and brings us back into fellowship with Him. Abandoning His unholy, imperfect children is unthinkable to God—just as it was unheard of to the father of the prodigal son. The apostle Paul writes, "You are all children of God through faith, for all of you who were baptized into Christ have clothed yourselves with Christ" (Galatians 3:26–27). Christ wraps us in His holiness, and when we come into God's presence we are protected. It's as if Jesus exposed Himself to the fiery heat of God's holiness and justice to take the punishment for us.

✳ *Work It Out:* *How can we prevent destruction? Where's our hope?*

• **Pray: "Jesus, I want to know You and grow closer to You."** Ask Him to guard your heart from mistruths about Him and to help you encounter Him in Scripture.

→ NOTES FOR GROWTH

A Key Point I Learned Today:

_____

_____

_____

How I Want to Grow:

_____

_____

_____

My Prayer List:

_____

_____

_____

DAY 20:

A RARE GLIMPSE AT GOD

While he was still speaking, a bright cloud covered them, and a voice from the cloud said, "This is my Son, whom I love; with him I am well pleased.
Listen to him!"
— Matthew 17:5

→ SEE HIM

The Transfiguration of Jesus

Jesus leads Peter, James, and John to a high mountain to pray. As He launches into a fervent prayer conversation with His Heavenly Father, the disciples fall asleep.

Sometime later, they stir in their sleep, and while only half-awake, they see Christ's entire appearance change as He prays.

Christ's face shines like the sun, and His clothes are as white as the light. Suddenly, Moses and Elijah appear and talk with Jesus.

Peter speaks up: "Lord, it is good for us to be here. If you wish, I will put up three shelters—one for you, one for Moses and one for Elijah."

As he speaks, a bright cloud envelopes them, and a voice from the cloud says, "This is my Son, whom I love; with him I am well pleased. Listen to him!"

The disciples fall face down on the ground—terrified. But Jesus touches them. "Get up," He says. "Don't be afraid."

They look up and see no one except Jesus.

As they come down the mountain, Jesus says, "Don't

tell anyone what you have seen, until the Son of Man has been raised from the dead." Matthew 17:9.

→ HEAR HIM

Explore the Word: Matthew 17:1–19

Talk about a mountaintop experience! Since they were part of Jesus' inner circle, Peter, James, and John had a front-row seat to all the action. And any doubts they had about Christ's true identity were swallowed up in that heavenly cloud. . .right?

Well, not quite.

When Jesus said, "The Son of Man is going to be betrayed into the hands of men," the disciples didn't understand what He was talking about. (See Mark 9:32.) What's more, some of them still thought Jesus was a prophet—an incredibly amazing one, but still just a prophet. After all, they witnessed Him doing the supernatural things prophets do: preaching, teaching, healing. . .performing miracles. And since two famous prophets showed up with Jesus, they naturally assumed He was among His equals—"divine peers" so to speak. As amazing as it may seem to us, the disciples still didn't make the connection that Jesus was the Messiah.

It's easy to point a finger and say, "How dense can they be? They've had all these intimate, face-to-face moments with Jesus—and yet they still don't get it!"

Honestly. . .we're not so different.

Think about the many blessings we receive from the Lord, the mountains He's helped us climb, the valleys He has walked us through. And then there are countless unseen interventions in the spiritual realm. Yet when we face seasons of struggle, we don't always remember the wisdom of the psalmist: "Be still and know that I am God" (Psalm

46:10). Sometimes we doubt and question God. Sometimes we feel abandoned by Him and wonder if He has the power to deliver us from our afflictions.

All along, the Messiah is standing next to us. "This is my Son, whom I love," God is telling us, "with him I am well pleased. Listen to him!"

Trust Him!

→ KNOW HIM

• **Defeat doubt before it defeats you.** Life can be tricky. There are so many things trying to get our attention. It's easy to get confused and make bad decisions. But we must stay focused on God and diligently seek His ways. "Have faith in God," Jesus answered. "I tell you the truth, if anyone says to this mountain, 'Go, throw yourself into the sea,' and does not doubt in his heart but believes that what he says will happen, it will be done for him. Therefore I tell you, whatever you ask for in prayer, believe that you have received it, and it will be yours" (Mark 11:22-24).

> ✳ *Work It Out: Are there guidelines for what you can ask for in prayer?*

• **Remember**—God sees the big picture. If we don't know God, it is easy to look for truth in the things of this world. We will always be disappointed when we rely on anyone other than God. "Trust in the Lord forever, for the Lord God is an everlasting rock." Isaiah 26:4.

> ✳ *Work It Out: How does God's power affect my personal life? In what ways can we connect with God's power?*

• Pray: **"Lord, please help me to recognize Your true identity. Open my eyes to the ways You want to help me every day."** Ask Him to help you not miss His work in your life.

→ NOTES FOR GROWTH

A Key Point I Learned Today:

_____

_____

_____

How I Want to Grow:

_____

_____

_____

My Prayer List:

_____

_____

_____

DAY 21:

DIVINE SPIT. . .ETERNAL SIGHT

*"As long as it is day, we must do the works of him who
sent me. Night is coming, when no one can work. While I
am in the world, I am the light of the world." After saying
this, he spit on the ground, made some mud with the
saliva, and put it on the man's eyes. "Go," he told him,
"wash in the Pool of Siloam" (this word means "Sent").
So the man went and washed, and came home seeing.*
— John 9:4–7

→ See Him

Washed Clean at the Pool of Siloam

His day begins like any other: begging for a scrap of food or
a cup of water, listening to the sounds of the world rushing
by, feeling his way to an invisible corner where he can just
disappear. No support. No kindness. No hope.

Darkness. That's all the blind man has never known.
Born this way, and destined to die as a lonely outcast.
Scratching out a miserable existence as a second-class
citizen—or as those in the Holy City have labeled him, "a
sinner."

So it comes as no surprise when a certain question
sticks in his ears from a group of men passing by: "Rabbi,
who sinned, this man or his parents, that he was born
blind?"

The answer changes everything. "Neither this man nor
his parents sinned, but this happened so that the work of
God might be displayed in his life."

That voice! The blind man detects a tone of compassion and love in each word—two things he's not used to receiving. And then the unexpected. Moistened fingertips gently massage his eyes.

"Go," that same voice commands, "wash in the Pool of Siloam."

The man gets up and makes his way to Jerusalem's most famous pool. He dips his hands in the cool water and frantically drenches his face. As the last bit of mud rolls off his cheek, his eyelids begin to flutter and he blinks a few times.

Suddenly, *light*!

It's painful at first, but then it quickly turns beautiful. *Glorious!* Colors and shapes come into focus. He sees the sunlight shimmering on water. He turns and locks eyes with people; faces of friends and family he has never before seen.

Can it really be true? The man I met has the power to bring light to my darkened eyes?

→ HEAR HIM

Explore the Word: John 9:1–41

Bible scholars who analyze this story often have a lot to say about the mud Jesus puts on this beggar's eyes. They describe it as a reminder of God's creation of man out of clay, and they point out that the Pharisees would consider the making of mud (mixing the spittle and dirt) to be work and unlawful on the Sabbath.

While each of these points may be true, I (Arnie) can't help thinking about Christ's humanity in this miracle. Each time I read this passage, I'm struck by a mind-boggling truth: *Jesus is fully man and fully God.*

Sadly, though, far too many people are willing to believe

one or the other, but not both. Just flip through the average illustrated children's Bible and you'll understand what I'm talking about. Too often, Jesus is depicted as a smiling, blue-eyed, blond-bearded "youth pastor-ish" surfer dude. (Few artists present Him as a guy's guy—the type who would actually...well, spit.)

But Jesus spat. And that's not all. He burped, He laughed. He probably got the hiccups. Jesus also was spat upon, and felt pain when He was beaten, whipped, and crucified.[1] Yet His "humanity" was able to do some pretty amazing things. He was able to heal people because Jesus is not just fully man, He is fully God.

That's why His spit, His touch, His word, could do amazing things.

He could heal every affliction, even death itself. He never sinned in word, action or thought. After He died, He came back to life. (Scripture does record Jesus spitting one last time. In Revelation 3:16, He spits out those who are lukewarm in their love for Him.)

Go back and reread today's passage, and think about this: Jesus experienced life as we do. But He is also God, so you can talk to Him at any time about what's going on in your life. And you can trust that He will understand. (Why not talk to Him right now?)[2]

→ Know Him

• **Never try to fit Jesus into your image of how the Messiah should look and act.** That's what the Jewish priests did. Men who had committed their lives to studying the scriptures and to seeking God's Son, actually met Jesus face-to-face—yet they rejected Him. Imagine that! They distrusted Jesus because He didn't fit their human definition of how the Messiah should look and behave. Just as we said back

---

1. See Matthew 26:67; 27:30.

2. Freelance writer Dean Anderson of Healdsburg, Calif., contributed to today's devotional entry.

in Day 19, focus on what scripture says about the Lord, not your impressions or mistruths about him.

> ✻ *Work It Out: When you talk to others about Jesus, how do you describe Him?*

• **Embrace the mystery of the Trinity.** Think about this: we have one God, but He's three Persons. Author and scholar James Montgomery Boice explains it this way in his book *The Sovereign God:* "If you hold out your hand and look at it, each of these three things is present. There is light, because it is only by light that you can see your hand. . . . There is also heat between your head and your hand. You can prove it by holding out a thermometer. It will vary as you go from a cold room to a warm room or from the outside to indoors. Finally, there is air. You can blow on your hand and feel it. You can wave your hand and thus fan your face."[3] Boice points out that while light, heat, and air are distinct from each other, it is impossible to have any one without the others (at least in an earthly setting). They are three and yet they are one.

> ✻ *Work It Out: Read John 1:14 and then share in your own words how Jesus is fully divine and fully human and the second Person of the Godhead.*

• **Pray: "Jesus, I know that You are the one and only triune God—the Father, the Son, and the Holy Spirit; I believe this, not because I understand it, but because the Bible teaches it and the Holy Spirit testifies in my heart to this truth."** Ask Jesus to help you explain this truth to others.

---

3. James Montgomery Boice, *The Sovereign God* (Downers Grove.: InterVarsity Press, 1978), 141–42.

→ NOTES FOR GROWTH

A Key Point I Learned Today:

_____

_____

_____

How I Want to Grow:

_____

_____

_____

My Prayer List:

_____

_____

_____

JESUS IS THE
GOOD SHEPHERD

DAY 22:

ONE FLOCK, ONE SHEPHERD

"I am the good shepherd; I know my sheep and my sheep know me—just as the Father knows me and I know the Father—and I lay down my life for the sheep."
—John 10:14–15

→ SEE HIM

Trusting the Good Shepherd

There is no better picture of Jesus' deep love and total commitment to us than the illustration of a shepherd. The life of a dedicated shepherd means total devotion to his flock—a devotion that includes putting the lives of the sheep above his own.

First of all, there are thieves and robbers—dishonest men who try to lure stray lambs away from the flock and steal them. They aren't interested in the animals' welfare; they're only interested in the money they can get from them.

Sound familiar? Unfortunately there are more than a few of those folks around today—people who have turned Christianity into the business of bucks instead of the commitment of love.

But Jesus makes it clear that if we honestly seek God, we'll eventually be able to tell His voice from the crooks'.

Second, there are plenty of wild animals—mostly wolves. Whenever they close in, fierce and ravenous from hunger, the hired hands usually split. Why should they risk their lives for somebody else's property?

But the committed shepherd never looks upon his

flock as "property." He's grown to know and love each of the sheep as individuals. In fact, his love and dedication to them are so intense that he would actually fight to the death to protect them.

Then there is the hazardous terrain on which the sheep graze—a dangerous landscape of holes, cliffs, and ravines. Knowing these pitfalls, the caring shepherd never pushes or drives his flock. Instead, he walks ahead of them, carefully scouting out the safest routes—gently leading them in areas he has already checked out.

Good pasture is also important. Grazing is about the only thing the sheep do, so why not make it as pleasant for them as possible? A sensitive shepherd goes to great risks to find the best grazing land for his sheep—to make their lives as happy and full as possible.

And finally, there are the hillside pens—places where the animals can gather for protection during the night. To make sure the sheep are really safe, the shepherd sleeps on the ground at the entrance of the pen. He will literally act as a human gate—a gate that serves as the only means to reach the flock.

→ HEAR HIM

Explore the Word: John 10:1–21

By comparing Himself to a good shepherd, Jesus promises to care for us with a tender, intense, and all-giving love: He will protect us from evil, He will fight off any enemy that's trying to destroy us, He will go before us in every situation, and He will give us a happy and full life.

And guess what? As Christians, the Lord wants us to share this same kind of radical love with the world. How?

It's Christ in us and the outpouring of His love through our words, our warmth, and our walk that will help others turn from evil. It's the Hero reflected in our faces who will open their eyes to eternity. "God desires to take our faces," writes Max Lucado, "this exposed and memorable part of our bodies, and use them to reflect His goodness."

→ Know Him

• **Get a clue about how love is supposed to be expressed:** "Love is patient, love is kind. It does not envy, it does not boast, it is not proud. It does not dishonor others, it is not self-seeking, it is not easily angered, it keeps no record of wrongs. Love does not delight in evil but rejoices with the truth. It always protects, always trusts, always hopes, always perseveres. Love never fails" (1 Corinthians 13:4–8).

> ✳ *Work It Out: Are you sharing God's love with those around you? What do people see when they look at your life? Humility, kindness, goodness— a reflection of Christ's face?*

• **Show kindness in your words and actions.** Best-selling author Frank Peretti, a man who considers himself to be among the world's "walking wounded," warns Christians about verbal abuse: "It's like painting a sign around your neck: 'Beat up on me because you'll get away with it.' You begin to expect to be treated that way, and the other kids pick up on that like an animal smelling prey. That's how it was for me. My teen world was a virtual prison. Here's some advice for Christians of all ages: Have nothing to do with words that wound."[1]

> ✳ *Work It Out: Tell how you strive to communicate hope through the things you do or say. Think of someone in your life who is hurting. Now share how you are going to reach out to this person.*

---

1. Interviewed by Tom Neven, "Teenage Torture," *Breakaway*, (October 2002), 6.

• Pray: "Lord, teach me how to share the love I experience through You with my friends—just as Christ 'laid down His life for His friends.'" Ask Him to use your speech and actions as a clear message of God's salvation, grace, and love.

→ NOTES FOR GROWTH

A Key Point I Learned Today:

_____

_____

_____

How I Want to Grow:

_____

_____

_____

My Prayer List:

_____

_____

_____

DAY 23:

"LAZARUS, COME FORTH!"

**Jesus, once more deeply moved, came to the tomb.
It was a cave with a stone laid across the entrance.
"Take away the stone," he said.**
—John 11:38–39

→ SEE HIM

"I Am the Resurrection and the Life"

Jesus feels upset as he approaches the tomb of Lazarus. It is a simple cave in the hillside with a slab of stone across the entrance. His dear friend is on the other side of the barrier—his heart no longer beating; his body cold in the tomb.

"Remove the stone," Jesus orders.

"The sister of the dead man, Martha, [says], "Master, by this time there's a stench. He's been dead four days!"[1]

Jesus commands, "Lazarus, come forth!" And Lazarus does! It's another example of the Lord's power over life and death. (Raising someone from the dead wasn't a one-time thing for Jesus; Jesus brought at least four different people back from the dead during His three-year ministry.)

Jesus looks Martha in the eye. "Did I not tell you that if you believe, you will see the glory of God?"[2] Jesus' other promises ring true at this moment:

"If you believe, you will receive whatever you ask for in prayer."[3]

"Everything is possible for one who believes."[4]

---

1. John 11:39 MSG
2. John 11:40.
3. Matthew 21:22.
4. Mark 9:23.

Then the Lord says to the others, "Go ahead, take away the stone."

So they take away the stone and Jesus raises His eyes to heaven and prays, "Father, I thank you that you have heard me. I knew that you always hear me, but I said this for the benefit of the people standing here, that they may believe that you sent me" (John 11:41–42).

The Lord says in a loud voice, "'Lazarus, come out!'" And he [comes] out, a cadaver, wrapped from head to toe, and with a kerchief over his face."[5]

Jesus tells them, "Take off the grave clothes and let him go."

→ HEAR HIM

Explore the Word: John 11:17–44

Besides showing Jesus' power and proving He is who He says He is, how does raising people from the dead apply to the living?

Here's what I (Arnie) have learned about the ugly topic of death: It comes in many forms. We don't have to be lying in a grave to experience it.

We may be young and alive on the outside, but inside there may be parts of us that have already died—dreams shattered, hopes destroyed, and pieces of our lives broken and withered. And for many of us—myself included—those areas may seem just as impossible to resurrect and bring back to life as raising a four-day-old corpse.

At one point during my younger years, I actually lost hope to the point of not wanting to live anymore. Thankfully, I got through that dark period and eventually found hope in Jesus Christ.

I learned that the first step to trusting Jesus is belief—especially that God can and will answer each of our prayers.

---

5. John 11:44 MSG

It also means believing that He may give us something far better than what we're asking for. . .or withhold from us something we only think we need. (I learned this lesson the hard way.)

You see, the Lord isn't a cosmic vending machine; someone we drop belief coins into and out pops the answers to our every whim. That would be only *partial* belief. *Full* belief involves trusting God more deeply. It involves trusting that if we ask for the wrong thing, God loves us enough to step in and give us what we really need instead. (What kind of love would He have for us if He always gave us what we *think* we need, instead of what He *knows* we need?)

In addition to trusting God, believing in Him, we must obey His guidance.

If Martha and Mary had not obeyed and had refused to roll the boulder away, it would have been a little tough for Lazarus to come out of the tomb. Obedience isn't always easy. The sisters were in a tough spot. After all, would you want to open up somebody's grave after he'd been rotting inside for four days? And what about their embarrassment if it didn't work out?

But they don't hesitate. Once they fully understand the Lord's command, they are willing to obey—even if it means looking foolish.[6]

→ KNOW HIM

• **Let go and trust God.** If you give up those strongholds of independence and let Him have control of them, you will be amazed at how He brings you to a better life than you thought possible.

---

6. A portion of this story was adapted from Bill Myers and Michael Ross, *Faith Encounter: Experience the Ultimate With Jesus* (Eugene, Oregon: Harvest House Publishers, 1999), 149-151.

✱ ***Work It Out:*** *What holds you back from surrendering yourself to Jesus?*

• **Be willing to believe and obey.** If you are willing, then the very thing you think is dead—the good that is rotting and seemingly impossible to save—will be given new and abundant life.

✱ ***Work It Out:*** *How obedient are we? Are we doing all that God asks of us? Or are there certain areas of our lives that we're still holding out on because we don't really trust Him or we are afraid we'll be disappointed? (Please explain your answer.)*

• **Pray: "Lord, fill my heart with the trust to know, truly know, that You are the stronghold in my life, always present, always available, no matter what."** Ask Him for the courage you need to surrender yourself to His will.

→ NOTES FOR GROWTH

A Key Point I Learned Today:

_____

_____

_____

How I Want to Grow:

_____

_____

_____

My Prayer List:

_____

_____

_____

DAY 24:

ROYAL WELCOME

> When they brought the colt to Jesus and threw their
> cloaks over it, he sat on it. Many people spread their
> cloaks on the road, while others spread branches they
> had cut in the fields. Those who went ahead and those
> who followed shouted, "Hosanna! Blessed is he who
> comes in the name of the Lord!"
> — Mark 11:7–9

→ SEE HIM

"Hosanna in the Highest!"

As Jesus approaches Jerusalem, He tells His disciples to
fetch an unridden donkey colt. (An unridden colt is often kept in a village for important visitors.) Jesus' disciples
know at once what He is saying by mounting this colt: He
is claiming to be the fulfillment of Zechariah 9:9:

> *Rejoice greatly, Daughter Zion! Shout,*
> *Daughter Jerusalem! See, your king comes to*
> *You, righteous and victorious, lowly and*
> *riding on a donkey, on a colt, the foal of a donkey.*

Jesus is announcing that He is coming to the capital as its
king.

The disciples envision the action: Jesus will ride in past
cheering crowds, ascend the temple steps, march into the
inner court, and grasp the horns at the corners of the altar.
This will signify that He is declaring His kingship. All the

people will rise against the Romans, and with the power of God behind them, the Jews will quickly oust the pagans and institute the kingdom of God.

(At least—that's what they think is happening.)

The crowds do cheer. They even fill the road with cloaks and tree branches to create a royal carpet. Christ is entering Jerusalem as King, but not quite the kind the Jews imagined. As they will soon discover, He isn't coming as a political leader; He is coming as the *spiritual King*.[1]

→ Hear Him

Explore the Word: Mark 11:1–11

The next time Jesus comes, He'll come as King of the physical world. But this first time He came to conquer Satan and become ruler of our hearts, minds, and souls—and to give us ultimate love.

As Christians we need to recognize that Satan is our enemy, but he's an enemy of Christ defeated on the cross. Even though we have victory in Jesus, the battle here on earth isn't over yet. Even though we are children of the King, Satan will do anything he can to trip us up.

But we have power through Jesus. We can stand strong against the devil and never cower or panic. Memorize this verse and hold on to its truth the next time you feel the heat of spiritual warfare: "You, dear children, are from God and have overcome them, because the one who is in you is greater than the one who is in the world" (1 John 4:4).

→ Know Him

• **Start living again by following Christ in a new direction.** Author Frank C. Laubach describes this as an awakening experience:

---

1. A portion of this story was adapted from Bill Myers and Michael Ross, *Faith Encounter: Experience the Ultimate With Jesus* (Eugene Harvest House Publishers, 1999), 155-156.

Has God ever struck you as the Great Stirrer-Up? One thing He seems to have determined is that we shall not fall asleep. We make or discover paradises for ourselves, and these paradises begin to lull us into sleepy satisfaction. Then God comes with His awakening hand, takes us by the shoulders and gives us a thorough awakening.

And God knows we need it. If our destiny is to grow on and on and on, into some far more beautiful creatures than we are now, with more of the ideals of Christ, that means that we need to have the shells broken quite frequently so that we can grow.[2]

✳ ***Work It Out:*** *Why is a spiritual awakening from Jesus the key to spiritual growth? Do you feel spiritually alive—or dead? (Please explain your answer.)*

• **Make the single most important decision you'll ever make in your life: Choose salvation through Jesus Christ.** Growing our relationship with Jesus is the daily pursuit of a forgiven life. His grace is free. But as we acknowledge our brokenness we allow God to work in our hearts on a deeper level than we ever imagined. He moves right into our hurts, hopes, bitterness, love, selfishness, mistakes, desires—name the issue and Christ is going to work in that part of our life. Consider this: He is the only One who truly knows our private thoughts and struggles.

✳ ***Work It Out:*** *Name some roadblocks to growth that you need Jesus to remove.*

---

2. Frank C. Laubach, *Letters by a Modern Mystic* (Grand Rapids: Revell, 1958), 47–48.

• **Pray: "Lord, I acknowledge You as the King of my life. Awaken me to new life in You."** Ask Jesus to remove the roadblocks to spiritual growth.

→ NOTES FOR GROWTH

A Key Point I Learned Today:

_____

_____

_____

How I Want to Grow:

_____

_____

_____

My Prayer List:

_____

_____

_____

DAY 25:

TIME TO CLEAR THE TEMPLE!

**On reaching Jerusalem, Jesus entered the temple courts
and began driving out those who were buying and
selling there. He overturned the tables of the money
changers and the benches of those selling doves, and
would not allow anyone to carry merchandise through
the temple courts. And as he taught them, he said, "Is it
not written: 'My house will be called a house of prayer
for all nations'? But you have made it 'a den of robbers.'"**
— Mark 11:15–17

→ SEE HIM

Jesus Exposes the Hearts of the "Religious" Leaders

The Lord is back in Jerusalem and decides to visit the temple. He makes the long trek up a series of crowded walkways and staircases that pass through tunnels and eventually open to a massive outer courtyard, the one called the Court of the Gentiles.

Before Jesus came to earth, King Herod the Great had expanded the temple, enclosing this area with colonnades and designating it as a place of prayer and worship for Gentiles (or non-Jews). And through the years, people from other lands have gravitated here.

While the entire thirty-five-acre complex is considered holy, it becomes increasingly more sacred as visitors move farther into the temple, from east to west. Yet non-Jews are strictly forbidden to go beyond the Court of the Gentiles. Warning signs in Greek and Latin are placed everywhere.

Their penalty for setting foot in the inner chambers: *death.*[1]
(The Romans have permitted the Jewish authorities to carry out executions for this offense, even if the offender is a Roman citizen.)[2]

So Jesus decides to visit this popular spot. But one glimpse and the Lord grimaces. His heart breaks by what it has become under the high priest, Caiaphas.

The courtyard is mobbed with people buying and selling animals—cattle, fowl, sheep—all for sacrifice at high prices because it is a cartel. Vendors are changing common currency for the coinage in which offerings have to be made, the shekel—which is another monopoly.[3] (These merchants make up to 1,800 percent!)

Only someone blind and deaf can pray in this bedlam.[4] It looks more like a hectic bazaar controlled by unscrupulous, self-serving men—not a sanctuary that honors God.

So in the very place that is the symbolic center of the nation, Jesus single-handedly drives out those who are selling animals for sacrifice and overturns—quite violently—the tables of the money changers. He evacuates the vendors who sell doves, stampedes the livestock out of the courtyard, and temporarily shuts down operations.

And then Jesus sits down calmly and begins to teach a stunned audience about God's holy temple:

It is to be a house of prayer for all nations (Mark 11:7).

It is the light of the nations, the place to which all people will come to acknowledge God (Isaiah 56:7–8).

It is a place of holiness, humility, honesty, truth, and sincere repentance before God—not a "den of robbers," not a place that can be manipulated by religious phonies (Mark 11:17).

It is Jesus' body; as the Son of God, He is the Temple (John 2:21–22).

---

1. See Bible History Online, http://www.biblehistory.com/jewishtemple/JEWISH_TEMPLE-The_Court_of_the_Gentiles.htm (accessed Ki;u 18. 2014).
2. Ibid.
3. See Karen C. Hinckley, *The Story of Stories: The Bible in Narrative Form* (Colorado Springs: NavPress, 1991), 234.
4. Ibid.

→ HEAR HIM

Explore the Word: Mark 11:12–33

Until now, Jesus had clashed mainly with the lay leaders of Judaism—the Pharisees and teachers of the law. But now He had challenged the chief priests, whose families probably owned the businesses Jesus had just shut down.[5]

Let's turn once again to insights from biblical scholar Craig G. Bartholomew, PhD, regarding today's passage:

> *When we see Jesus' cleansing of the temple in this context [that He is the Temple], it becomes clear why the Jewish leaders begin to look for a way to kill him. Not only is he challenging their treasured hopes and aspirations and announcing the destruction of their most cherished symbol. He also is doing these things in the name of the Lord, their God! He is acting as if He is God's chosen Messiah. Though the Pharisees, Sadducees, and others who vie to lead Israel can agree on nothing else, they do agree that this man Jesus threatens their whole way of life with his claim of the coming kingdom. This man has to go!*[6]

After the housecleaning, people began grilling Jesus about who He thought He was. Pulling off the stunt He did called for some pretty high authority. If He was claiming to be the Christ, then He had better get to it and make His point by impressing everyone with a few miracles.

But God wouldn't be bullied.

He will *never* be manipulated.

Jesus' miracles are for loving, healing, and encouraging. They are never meant to entertain the curious. So instead of putting on a sideshow, the Lord prophesied about His

---

5. Ibid.
6. Bartholomew and Goheen, *Drama of Scripture,* 157.

upcoming resurrection. But, as was usually the case with spiritual truth, the people missed the boat. They thought He was talking about an immediate, literal interpretation: "You claim You can rebuild our temple in how many days?"

They didn't expect His deeper, change-all-the-rules, eternal truth: "In three days I'll raise this temple, My body, from the dead to prove I'm telling the truth about Myself. I'll be doing this to demonstrate a purer, more powerful form of worship—a worship in which God will no longer be living inside a temple, but will actually be living inside of people."

→ Know Him

• **Never forget who Jesus is—the righteous God.** One day, every one of us will stand in His presence and give an account for our lives. "It is a dreadful thing to fall into the hands of the living God" (Hebrews 10:31). Author John G. Mitchell makes this connection with Jesus' actions in the temple and how it applies to our lives today: "Christ cleansed the temple when men sinned and made it unclean. Similarly, the Lord has a right to cleanse us when we sin. It is much better for us to willingly confess our sins so that He may forgive and cleanse us. And He is willing and ready to do just that. How wonderful it is to know that the blood of Jesus Christ, God's Son, cleanses us from all sin (see 1 John 1:7)."[7]

> ✳ *Work It Out: Based on today's lesson, tell in your own words what the temple merchants, as well as the chief priests, did that made Jesus upset. How does this relate to your life—and the life of your church community?*

---

7. This quote is taken from *Time with God: The New Testament for Busy People* (Dallas: Word Publishing, 1991), 227.

• **Be holy "as Christ is holy."** *Holiness.* It's one of those words that brings to mind a long list of rigid, narrow-minded rules that are out of touch with reality—not to mention completely out of reach. Yet consider this: Scripture says, "Make every effort to live in peace with everyone and to be holy; without holiness no one will see the Lord" (Hebrews 12:14). At times, our lives stray far away from anything that remotely resembles holiness. And the truth is, no one is born holy. So what's a weak, imperfect Christian to do? Turn to Christ for help. Take a look at what *The Message* says: "Here it is in a nutshell: Just as one person did it wrong and got us in all this trouble with sin and death, another person did it right and got us out of it. But more than just getting us out of trouble, he got us into life! (Romans 5:18–19).

✳ ***Work It Out:*** *What does it mean to be holy? How can we live out holiness in practical ways?*

• **Pray:** "**Lord, help me to have a pure heart before You—and to honor You with my body.**" Ask Him to cleanse your motives.

→ NOTES FOR GROWTH

A Key Point I Learned Today:

_____

_____

_____

How I Want to Grow:

_____

_____

_____

My Prayer List:

_____

_____

DAY 26:

THE MASTER SERVES
HIS SERVANTS

Jesus knew that the Father had put all things under his power, and that he had come from God and was returning to God; so he got up from the meal, took off his outer clothing, and wrapped a towel around his waist. After that, he poured water into a basin and began to wash his disciples' feet, drying them with the towel that was wrapped around him.
—John 13:3–5

→ SEE HIM

Take Up the Towel of Servanthood

Jewish custom calls for the host's servant to wash the guests' feet.

But since there is no host where Jesus and His friends are eating, there is no servant. (Other Gospel accounts talk about how the disciples have been arguing over which of them is the greatest—so there's a good chance most of them are pretty worried about who's going to end up with the bottom-of-the-barrel job of feet washing.)

But what does Jesus do?

He gets up from the meal, takes off His outer clothing, and wraps a towel around His waist. Then He pours water in a basin and begins washing each of the disciples' feet.

Pause right there and study that mental picture for a moment.

God—the Creator of the heavens and the earth and every man, woman, and child who has ever (and will ever) populate this world—kneels and begins washing the sweaty, dirty feet of His followers.

Jesus comes to Simon Peter, who asks, "Lord, are You going to wash my feet?"

Jesus replies, "You do not realize now what I'm doing, but later you will understand."

"No," Peter insists. "You shall never wash my feet."

Jesus answers, "Unless I wash you, you have no part with Me."

→ HEAR HIM

Explore the Word: John 13:1–17

What a perfect picture. What a perfect example of God's heart—of the depth of His love and commitment to each of us.

It is also a perfect demonstration of what God considers to be real greatness. It's not found in the world leaders, the professional athletes, the Hollywood superstars. It's not even found in the great spiritual leaders of our times. These aren't the ones whom God considers to be great. Instead, according to the Lord, "whoever wants to become great among you must be your servant, and whoever wants to be first must be your slave—just as the Son of Man did not come to be served, but to serve."[1]

Here's what author Henri J. M. Nouwen says about Christ's example of servanthood:

---

1. Matthew 20:26–28.

After washing His disciples' feet, Jesus says, "I have given you an example so that you may copy what I have done to you" (John 13:15). After giving Himself as food and drink, He says, "Do this in remembrance of Me" (Luke 22:19). Jesus calls us to continue His mission of revealing the perfect love of God in this world. He calls us to total self-giving. He does not want us to keep anything for ourselves. Rather, He wants our love to be as full, as radical, and as complete as His own. He wants us to bend ourselves to the ground and touch the places in each other that most need washing. He also wants us to say to each other, "Eat of me and drink of me." By this complete mutual nurturing, He wants us to become one body and one spirit, united by the love of God.

Are you ready for true greatness? Take some clues from Jesus and reach out to others as a servant.

→ Know Him

• **Take the time to look around you.** Someone needs you. Someone at church, at school, at home. There's that seventy-four-year-old man whose wife has Alzheimer's disease—he needs someone to talk to. Then there's that couple with a handicapped child—they really could use a break. You don't have to head off on a mission trip to Panama to serve God. Do it every day. . .in lots of little ways.

✳ *Work It Out: List ways you can serve your church community.*

• **Be Christ's hands and feet.** From His birth to His death on a cross, Jesus' life was a shining example of humility and service. He reached out to those whom no one else wanted around. He brought love to the unloved, hope to the hopeless. How about you?

> ✳ *Work It Out: Ask God to help you find at least one non-Christian person you can reach—through prayer as well as service. Make a list right now, and then take action.*

• **Pray: "Lord, break me and use me in ways that stretch way beyond my imagination."** Ask Jesus to help you get out of your comfort zone for a couple of weeks.

→ NOTES FOR GROWTH

A Key Point I Learned Today:

_____
_____
_____

How I Want to Grow:

_____
_____
_____

My Prayer List:

_____
_____
_____

DAY 27:

THE LAST SUPPER

**While they were eating, Jesus took bread, and when he
had given thanks he broke it and gave it to his disciples,
saying, "Take and eat; this is my body."**
— Matthew 26:26

→ SEE HIM

Jesus Offers Spiritual Food

The twelve men in the upper room with Jesus know every
detail of the Passover celebration; they've learned it from a
lifetime of annual rituals.[1]

First, there is a candlelight search for any leaven (yeast)
in the house, and all leaven found is removed. Then they
gather around a low table. Every bit of food set out before
them is symbolic: parsley represents life that is created by
God; the salt water it is dipped in reminds them of the
tears shed during bondage—and so do the bitter herbs; the
unleavened bread recalls the haste with which the Israelites left Egypt; four cups of wine punctuate the dinner at
intervals and are symbols of the fourfold expression of the
Lord's promised deliverance: the Cup of Sanctification, the
Cup of Judgment, the Cup of Redemption, and the Cup
of Praise.

Carefully stipulated hand washing is meticulously followed, and the story of the Passover in Egypt is retold:

> *". . .Eat it in haste; it is the Lord's Passover. On that
> same night I will pass through Egypt and strike
> down every firstborn of both people and animals,*

---

1. See Anderson, *Jesus*, 294.

*and I will bring judgment on all the gods of Egypt.
I am the LORD. The blood will be a sign for you on
the houses where you are, and when I see the blood, I
will pass over you. No destructive plague will touch
you when I strike Egypt. This is a day you are to
commemorate; for the generations to come you shall
celebrate it as a festival to the LORD—a lasting
ordinance" (Exodus 12:11–14).*

But during tonight's Passover meal, something is missing.

Usually positioned next to the other symbolic elements is a roasted lamb. This meat, cooked exactly the way God had instructed in Exodus, signifies the sacrifice whose blood protected Jewish homes from the destroyer. But the official lambs are not to be sacrificed until tomorrow afternoon, and only by temple priests.[2] And besides, Jesus intends for this meal to be different. He knows it's about to become one of the most memorable nights of the disciples' lives.

As He blesses the bread, He breaks it and gives it to each man, telling them, "Take. Eat. This is My body."

And then He raises the cup, thanks God for it, and offers it to them. "Drink this, all of you. This is My blood, God's new covenant poured out for many people for the forgiveness of sins."

Suddenly, a serious tone washes over the meal. *What did He say? Sins are forgiven through. . .the Rabbi's blood?*

"I will not drink of this fruit of the vine from now on," Jesus continues, "until that day when I drink it anew with you in My Father's kingdom."

Jesus goes on to explain that He is leaving and that in His absence the apostles will face fierce opposition from the world. But they needn't feel fearful or abandoned, because someone called the *Parakletos*—the Comforter, Counselor,

---

2. See Hinckley, *Story of Stories,* 235–36.

Helper—will come to their aid.[3] This was the Spirit who had inspired the prophets and who had been enabling Jesus to do His works of power.

But the disciples are uneasy and have more questions with each answer Jesus gives them. *Where is Jesus going? Why can't we come too?*

→ HEAR HIM

Explore the Word: Matthew 26:17–30

Imagine sitting at the table with Jesus—fully knowing what's about to happen (unlike the disciples.) His death seems so close, so real. Your heart is breaking.

Jesus then takes a piece of bread, breaks it apart, and says, "Take and eat, this is My body." And a cup. He gives thanks and says, "Drink from it, all of you."

How can you go through with this, Lord?

"This is My blood of the covenant, which is poured out for many for the forgiveness of sins."

And it's not just sin in general. Your sins! My sins! That's a sobering thought. That darkest, most depressing day for our Lord—for you, for me.[4]

How can someone love another that much?

How can He lay down His life. . .for me?

As I (Michael) read this passage of scripture, my mind goes back to John the Baptist's description of Jesus (see John 1:29–31). What does he call the Holy One? *The "Lamb of God"!*

Sounds strange to the ear, yet John knew the truth about Jesus, and he didn't want anyone to miss it. A lamb was used in the temple sacrifice to pay for the sins of humans. Every day a lamb was killed in the morning, then another in the evening.

Some pretty amazing symbolism. It's Jesus' blood that

---

3. Ibid., 236.

4. Dirk R. Buursma, *Daylight Devotional Bible* (Grand Rapids: Zondervan, 1988), 1049.

saves us from eternal death. So in one sense, John is saying, "Look, this is the lamb that God has supplied—this is the One who will suffer and die in our place for all our sins. He will take all of your sins—every failure, everything you've ever done wrong—and dispose of them forever. He will take all that guilt, all that blame upon Himself. He will take the punishment that should be yours so you can be clean, so you can be free."

Think about this truth—these scenes—the next time you take communion.

→ KNOW HIM

• **Break bread through God's Word.** Bible engagement is an essential way in which God communicates with us. Without scripture, we wouldn't know (1) what God is like, (2) His plan for us, (3) how much He loves us, (4) the right way to live, or (5) anything about what will happen to us after we die. To grow in grace, we have to do more than casually read scripture. We need to feed on it, digest it. Here's how Eugene Peterson, author of *The Message*, explains Bible engagement: "Reading is an immense gift, but only if the words are assimilated, taken into the soul—eaten, chewed, gnawed, received in unhurried delight. Words of men and women long dead, or separated by miles and/or years, come off the page and enter our lives freshly and precisely, conveying truth and beauty and goodness, words that God's Spirit has used and uses to breathe life into our souls."[5]

> ✳ **Work It Out:** *As you read verses and whole passages of scripture, stop periodically and pray about what you are reading. Is there a promise to claim or a change to make in your life? Pray about it. Tell why this interactive, relational way of engaging God's Word is like "breaking bread" with Jesus.*

---

5. Eugene H. Peterson, *Eat This Book* (Grand Rapids: Eerdmans, , 2006), 10–11.

• **Break bread through praise and worship.** God wants our worship. It pleases Him, and it connects our lives to His heart, His power, His will. Read John 4:1–26 for some clues about the kinds of worshippers He seeks. (Hint: These verses talk about believers who worship God in *spirit* and in *truth*.) And what does Jesus offer? Living water. As for most Christians, our faith can get pretty dry at times. But the living water Jesus gives can transform the most desolate, desert-like soul into an abundant life spring! But be warned: If we don't make worship a priority, our Christian walk will be shallow and ineffective.

> ✳ ***Work It Out:*** *How would you describe your worship times—on fire. . .or as dead as a graveyard? What can you do to make worship a more meaningful experience?*

• **Pray: "Jesus, I want to *want* to focus on You during church and my personal study times. Work in my heart; deepen my faith."** Ask Jesus to prepare your heart *before* you step through the church doors.

→ NOTES FOR GROWTH

A Key Point I Learned Today:

_____

_____

_____

How I Want to Grow:

_____

_____

_____

My Prayer List:

_____

_____

_____

DAY 28:

A HEART-TO-HEART TALK

"Father, the hour has come. Glorify your Son, that your Son may glorify you. For you granted him authority over all people that he might give eternal life to all those you have given him. Now this is eternal life: that they know you, the only true God, and Jesus Christ, whom you have sent. I have brought you glory on earth by finishing the work you gave me to do. And now, Father, glorify me in your presence with the glory I had with you before the world began."
—John 17:1–5

→ See Him

Jesus Prays in the Garden

It's now Thursday evening, and at this point, Jesus is finished training His disciples. For months and months (some believe as long as three or more years), He has nurtured their faith and has equipped them for service in His kingdom. He has laughed with them, cried with them, and on countless occasions, He has broken bread with them.

Tonight, the Lord and His followers are in the Garden of Gethsemane, nestled at the bottom of the slope of Mount Olivet. Here, the rocky paths and groves of gnarled olive trees hold a special place in their hearts. It's a familiar meeting spot for the disciples. And once the sun disappears on the horizon, the lights of Jerusalem seem to pop up in nearly every direction. The view is almost mystical with the flickering of oil lanterns in the windows. The air is filled with the smoky scent of cooking fires, and there are the distant sounds of dogs barking and children playing.

The time has come for Jesus to fulfill what He was born to do, and He dreads what's next: torture and agony; unimaginable suffering as all the sins and wrongdoing of humanity are put on Him.

"Sit here while I pray," Jesus says. He takes Peter, James, and John down the path to the oil press. During the short walk, a dark cloud of sorrow and trouble falls over Jesus like a sudden storm on Galilee's lake.[1] "My soul is overwhelmed with sorrow to the point of death," he says. "Stay here and keep watch."

This prayer, more than any other in the Bible, captures the heart and deepest yearnings of Jesus. He lets the disciples (and us) eavesdrop on His most intimate conversation with His Father.

Jesus prays for Himself. First, He asks to be glorified "with the glory I had with you before the world began." Jesus is not on some power trip here. He knows that He is about to face more agony than any human being has ever faced in the history of the world—not just the pain of the cross, mind you, but the suffering and punishment for all the world's sins. For these few hours, He will literally carry the weight of the entire world on His shoulders.

And He knows one other thing that presses in on Him. Jesus knows He can back out and call it quits anytime He wants. So He prays for the strength and courage to go through with it, to succeed. If He does, there is no more perfect demonstration of God's love for us—or of His Son's immense glory.

Jesus prays for the disciples. Next, He prays for His friends. First, He asks for unity. It's as if He already knows the centuries of arguments and fights that are going to plague the church—everything from wars over major doctrines to hurt

---

1. Anderson, Jesus, 313..

feelings about what color the curtains in the church bathroom should be.

Then He prays that even though the world may hate them, His followers will have the "full measure" of His joy. Again Jesus makes it clear that real joy doesn't depend on outward circumstances. Real joy comes from the depth of our relationship with God.

Jesus prays for protection. Finally, He asks the Father to protect the disciples from the world. Not to take them out of the world—but to protect them while they're in it.

"Righteous Father," Jesus prays, "though the world does not know you, I know you, and they know that you have sent me. I have made you known to them, and will continue to make you known in order that the love you have for me may be in them and that I myself may be in them" (John 17:25–26).

→ Hear Him

Explore the Word: John 17:1–26

God hears and answers our prayers. But as Jesus demonstrates in the Garden, we must be proactive. We must open the window by kneeling before Him in prayer. Jesus says that we have not because we ask not. James tells us that the effectual, fervent prayer of a righteous person accomplishes much. Again and again, the scriptures reveal to us that prayer is an effective tool.

God delights in our prayers. He longs to demonstrate His power in the tremendous trials that shake the foundations of our lives, as well as in the tiny troubles that annoy us. Giant needs are never too great for His power; small ones are never too insignificant for His love.

God answers prayer because He is the supreme ruler of all. He governs both world events and our individual lives, ready at our request to act, to intervene, to overrule for our good, His glory, and the progress of the Gospel.

God moves through prayer. Not only are we called to this divine activity (Philippians 4:6 and 1 Timothy 2:1–3), but we are guaranteed of God's action in response to our prayers. And as 2 Chronicles clearly states, if we pray, God promises results. He has assured us that prayer is the way to secure His aid and to move His mighty hand. Therefore, even in sickness, failure, rejection, or financial distress, we can pray and experience His peace. "'Have faith in God,' Jesus answered. 'Truly I tell you, if anyone says to this mountain, 'Go, throw yourself into the sea,' and does not doubt in his heart but believes that what they say will happen, it will be done for them" (Mark 11:22–23).

Our Lord Jesus often slipped away to be alone and to pray. In her book *Jesus, Man of Prayer,* Margaret Magdalen writes: "Jesus needed the silence of eternity as a thirsting man in the desert needs water. . . . He longed for time apart to bask and sunbathe in His Father's love, to soak in it and repose in it. No matter how drained He felt, it seems that this deep, silent communion refreshed Him more than a good night's sleep."[2]

→ KNOW HIM

• **Pray through good times—and difficult seasons.** Our faith journey will take us through the many changing conditions of the soul. "We may not have expected things to get tougher before they get better," Denver Seminary professor and author Howard Baker points out. "Certainly, we did not expect to have our innermost selves exposed—our misgivings about God, our doubt, apathy, disillusionment, depression."[3]

2. Margaret Magdalen, *Jesus, Man of Prayer* (Downers Grove: InterVarsity Press, 1987), p. x.
3. Howard Baker, *Soul Keeping* (Colorado Springs: NavPress, 1998), 59.

✻ Work It Out: *Are you committed to prayer? Are you convinced that God's power moves through prayer? (Please explain your answer.)*

• **Pray through God's Word.** Jesus is our source of strength and hope. We need to be an active participant in this transformation from desolation and hopelessness to renewal and light—it doesn't just happen on its own. One of the ways we can begin this turn toward God is by returning to His Word day after day. He speaks a message crafted especially for each one of us there. We need only open the pages of His book to discover what that message is.

✻ Work It Out: *Tell why it's important to mix prayer and Bible engagement every day.*

• **Pray: "From this day forward, Lord, I will value my relationship with You. And like any relationship I value here on earth, I will work at deepening it and growing it, through prayer and Bible study."** Ask Him to show you how to pray.

→ NOTES FOR GROWTH

A Key Point I Learned Today:

_____

_____

_____

How I Want to Grow:

_____

_____

_____

My Prayer List:

_____

_____

_____

JESUS IS THE DELIVERER
AND REDEEMER

DAY 29:

JESUS IS ARRESTED

Now the betrayer had arranged a signal with them: "The one I kiss is the man; arrest him and lead him away under guard." Going at once to Jesus, Judas said, "Rabbi!" and kissed him. The men seized Jesus and arrested him.
— Mark 14:44–46

→ SEE HIM

Betrayed in Gethsemane

The horror of what Jesus is facing is so overpowering that He literally throws Himself to the ground, not once, but several times, begging the Father to find some other way. "Abba, Father," He says, "everything is possible for You. Take this cup from Me. Yet not what I will, but what You will."

Three times He pleads for the Father to call the whole thing off. He doesn't have to go through with this. He's innocent; He didn't foul up the world with sin—humans did. So why should He suffer? And yet there's His deep, deep love for humanity.

A tremendous, agonizing battle plays out. Three times the fate of the world hangs in the balance. Three times He nearly calls the whole thing off. The struggle is so intense and excruciating that tiny capillaries begin to explode near the surface of His skin, causing Him to sweat not only water but blood.[1]

And the final outcome?

Jesus' love is so great that He decides that He will lay down His life for mankind. Imagine that: God cares more

---
1. See Luke 22:44.

for our lives than for His own!

Suddenly, Jesus' prayer time is interrupted as Judas arrives with a detachment of Roman soldiers and officials from the chief priests and Pharisees. They are carrying torches, lanterns, and weapons.

Just to make it clear that He is cooperating under His own authority—not man's—Jesus announces His identity. "Who is it you want?"

"Jesus of Nazareth," they reply.

The power of that statement literally knocks everyone to the ground.[2] (The very men who are about to arrest and kill Jesus find themselves on their faces before Him.)

Peter grabs a sword and tries to fight off the soldiers, but only manages to hack off the right ear of the servant of the high priest. Jesus orders him to stop and heals the wounded man right on the spot.[3]

The Lord has come to do the will of our heavenly Father: to save and to heal—even those who are about to kill Him. Jesus gives Himself up without a struggle, *and* remains completely in control of the situation.[4]

→ HEAR HIM

Explore the Word: Mark 14:43–52

Here's what I (Arnie) have learned through my many years on planet Earth: Science and technology can't save us, and all the money in the world can't buy even one soul's entry into heaven. Our only hope is Jesus Christ and the price He paid on the cross—with His very life! It's up to us to believe and accept His eternal gift of salvation.

Relationship makes all the difference. More specifically, relationship with the one, true God of the Bible—not

2. See John 18:3–6.

3. See Luke 22:50–51.

4. A portion of this story was adapted from Bill Myers and Michael Ross, *Faith Encounter: Experience the Ultimate With Jesus* (Eugene Harvest House Publishers, 1999), 204-205.

your notion of who God is, but *the real God* who loves unconditionally, who is able to heal the soul in radical ways, who forgives completely. . .and who has found a way to move us from death to life.

But I'm not going to kid you: following Christ isn't easy. Real, lasting spiritual growth involves *movement*. Maybe it means crawling out of that pit you're in and shaking off the shame. I'm quite certain it will involve turning away from the countless lies you've been fed about faith, God, and growth. . .and walking day-by-day along a path that's grounded in something living and breathing. And it means admitting a few things: your flaws, frailties, frustrations—which you are safe to do in this trusting relationship of unconditional love.

→ KNOW HIM

• **Open your eyes to the future God wants to give you.** The Lord is calling you to set your sights on the wonderful life ahead. People who reject Him focus on what they are overcoming. Christ-followers focus on what they are becoming.

> ✳ **Work It Out:** *Who are you becoming in Christ? What is He helping you to overcome?*

• **Consider Christ's power.** Do you ever think Jesus is weak during those final days? Don't! He is the powerful Son of God who is in control of the entire universe. Consider this:
> ➢ He has power over His enemies.
> ➢ He has the power to lay down His life and the power to take it back again.
> ➢ He has the power to defeat Satan.
> ➢ He has the power to free us from sin.
> ➢ He has the power to create and to heal.
> ➢ He has the power to transform the lives of believers.

✳ *Work It Out: Are you relying on Christ's power? Do you believe He has the power to transform your life? (What's blocking the change?)*

• **Pray: "Jesus, please empower me."** Ask Him to deliver you from the sin that entangles your life.

→ NOTES FOR GROWTH

A Key Point I Learned Today:

_____

_____

_____

How I Want to Grow:

_____

_____

_____

My Prayer List:

_____

_____

_____

DAY 30:

TRUTH ON TRIAL

> The high priest said to him, "I charge you under
> oath by the living God: Tell us if you are the Messiah,
> the Son of God." "You have said so," Jesus replied.
> "But I say to all of you: From now on you will see
> the Son of Man sitting at the right hand of the
> Mighty One and coming on the clouds of heaven."
> — Matthew 26:63–64

→ See Him

Before the Jewish Court of Elders

It's daybreak, and Jesus has been brought before the Sanhedrin (powerful religious leaders). The high priest, Caiaphas, doesn't even pretend to hold a fair court, nor does he mask his hatred for the Lord. He's desperately clawing for the tiniest speck of evidence against Jesus so he can put Him to death. But so far, he can't find any.

"He consorts with sinners and tax collectors," someone yells to the crowd that has gathered in Caiaphas' palace. The high priest stares blankly, as if to dismiss the charge.

"He breaks the Sabbath law," another chimes in.

And still another speaks up: "He claims He can forgive sins."

"Noted. Noted. *Noted!*" Caiaphas raises his voice in procedural scorn. "We've heard it all before, and none of it warrants execution. Who brings against the defendant witness concerning a capital crime, an offense deserving death?"[1]

---

1. See Wangerin, *Book of God*, 791.

Suddenly, some in the room stand up and give false testimony against Jesus: "We heard Him say, 'I will destroy this man-made temple and in three days will build another, not made with hands.'" Yet even then their testimony does not agree.[2]

The high priest rises to his feet and glares at Jesus. "Are You not going to answer?" he thunders. "What is this testimony that these men are bringing against You?"

Jesus remains silent.

Caiaphas grows impatient: "Tell us if You are the Christ, the Son of God."

Jesus finally answers, "Yes, it is as you say."

The priest tears his clothes and accuses Jesus of speaking blasphemy. The other officials agree: "He is worthy of death."

They spit in Jesus' face and strike Him with their fists.

→ HEAR HIM

Explore the Word: Matthew 26:57–27:10

Imagine how alone Jesus must have felt. His friends doubted and even betrayed Him; the very people He came to save spit in His face. It never occurred to anyone that chilly morning that Christ's claims just might be true. Even though they had seen and witnessed His miracles—and despite the fact that they had marveled at His teachings—those who put Jesus on trial were spiritually blind. They refused to see the truth.

Still, two comforting facts emerge from today's hostile scene:

Jesus is who He claims to be. Therefore, we must acknowledge that He is Lord and give Him the glory and honor He deserves. Hebrews 1:3 tells us, "The Son is the radiance of God's glory and the exact representation of his being, sustaining all things by his powerful word." And Jesus said, "If

2. See Mark 14:57–59.

you've seen Me, you've seen the Father."

Jesus proves that He loves us wildly. He loves us despite our mixed-up hearts. He loves us when we shake our fists at Him and spit in His face. He loves us no matter what.

He loves us so much, *He* hurts when *we* hurt.

God's love is something no one can fully grasp. And because of it, He forgives our sin through Jesus Christ and graciously brings us back into fellowship with Him. Abandoning His unholy, imperfect children is unthinkable to God—just as it was unheard of to the father of the prodigal son.

It's this radical love that took Him to the cross.

→ KNOW HIM

• **Fear the Lord and honor His holy name.** There's a reason Christ-followers cringe when the world uses the Lord's name in vain. According to scripture, "The fear of the LORD is the beginning of wisdom" (Proverbs 9:10). John fell to his feet when God spoke to him (Revelation 1:17); Paul dropped to the ground when he encountered Jesus on the road to Damascus (Acts 9:4); Moses trembled when God spoke to him (Acts 7:32). Now contrast these acts of reverence with the hateful behavior of Caiaphas, the Sanhedrin, and the Roman guards. (Are you cringing yet?)

> ✳ *Work It Out: Consider how your own disobedience is like a "slap in the face" to our holy Lord. What must we do to nurture a right relationship with Jesus?*

• **Remember—God is faithful.** In the Lord's perfect time, He gives a new beginning to people who so easily turn their backs on Him; rebellious children who break promises; generations that know more than a little about disobedience—people like you and me. If today's study hasn't convinced you, turn to the book of Judges for more proof. It's filled with snapshot after snapshot of raw, uncensored *rebelliousness*—and God's gracious, divine deliverance.

"Then the Israelites did evil in the eyes of the LORD and served the Baals" (Judges 2:11). Keep reading and you'll discover that despite humankind's gross unfaithfulness, *God is faithful.* He molds and disciplines His children. He shows persistent, unwearied love and matchless grace; grace that's absolutely underserved.

> ✻ ***Work It Out:*** *List some ways that the Lord has been faithful in your life. Was there a time when His forgiveness seemed too good to be true; something you had a difficult time believing and accepting? (Explain your answer.)*

• **Pray: "Lord Jesus, I know I can find comfort in the fact that You will never turn your back on me."** Ask Jesus to show you how to lean on an old, familiar truth: " 'Be still, and know that I am God; I will be exalted among the nations, I will be exalted in the earth.' The LORD Almighty is with us; the God of Jacob is our fortress" (Psalm 46:10–11).

→ NOTES FOR GROWTH

A Key Point I Learned Today:

_____

_____

_____

How I Want to Grow:

_____

_____

_____

_____

My Prayer List:

_____

_____

_____

DAY 31:

THORNS, NAILS, AND A CROSS

"Here is your king," Pilate said to the Jews.
But they shouted, "Take him away! Take him away!
Crucify him!" "Shall I crucify your king?"
Pilate asked. "We have no king but Caesar,"
the chief priests answered. Finally Pilate handed
him over to them to be crucified.
—John 19:14-16

→ SEE HIM

Jesus Is Sentenced to Be Crucified

Since Israel is occupied by the Romans, the Jews have no say over who will live or die. So they've taken Jesus to the praetorium (the governor's headquarters) and have handed him over to the Roman in charge, Pontius Pilate. The Jews—who hate paying Roman taxes and who reluctantly acknowledge Tiberius Caesar as their king—won't enter the building, so the accusers are all outside.

Pilate is nervous.

His wife has recently had a troubling dream and warned him: "Don't have anything to do with that innocent man, for I have suffered a great deal today in a dream because of him."[1]

And to make matters worse, Jesus isn't an easy man to interrogate. Inside the praetorium, the governor is in his usual spot—the Seat of Judgment—but shifts uncomfortably in his chair.[2]

---

1. Matthew 27:19.
2. Charles B. Templeton, *Jesus* (New York: Simon & Schuster, 1973), 179.

Jesus is standing before him. Silent.

Pilate swallows and then asks point-blank, "Are You the king of the Jews?"

"Is that your own question," Jesus replies, "or did others suggest you ask Me that?" The Lord's response is not a diversion. Jesus is asking if Pilate is inquiring from a Jewish point of view—in which case the answer would be "yes"— or from a Roman perspective—in which case the answer would be "no."[3]

"What do you take me for?" Pilate responds. "Am I a Jew? Your chief priests and own people arrested you and brought you before me. The question is. . .why? What's your crime?"

"If I were the king of some country," Jesus responds, "my servants would have fought to keep Me from being arrested. But I am not—My kingdom is elsewhere."

"You *are* a king then?"

"Exactly as you say; I am. That's why I was born. That's why I came to the world—to be a witness for truth. And everyone on the side of truth heeds what I say."

It's an answer that gives Pilate a quiet sigh of relief. Yet he can't help feeling amazed at the powerful presence and sense of authority exuding from a prisoner under such pressure.[4]

"Truth," the governor says as he rises to his feet, "what's truth?" He then turns and heads outside to address the Sanhedrin and the crowd waiting with them.

As the morning drags on, Jesus is bounced from the praetorium on the northeast side of Jerusalem to the Palace of Herod on the west side of the city. . .and then back to Pilate. The governor doesn't find Jesus guilty of anything— not religious blasphemy, not corrupting the people, nor even political treason as the Sanhedrin claims. He wants to wash his hands of the whole ordeal and had hoped he could

---

3. Anderson, *Jesus,* 328–29.
4. Ibid., 329.

escape the conflict by sending Jesus across town. After all, the Man some believe is the Christ is from Galilee—and that's Herod Antipas's jurisdiction.

But the plan backfires.

Once again Pilate is standing face-to-face with Jesus. This time, the Lord is decked out in an elegant purple robe, the impressive clothes of a king. (It's Herod's little joke.) The governor is now certain that the chief priests had brought Jesus before him out of envy. But with the roar of the crowd growing louder—"Crucify Him!"—and pressure mounting from the Sanhedrin, Pilate gives in. He takes a basin of water and publicly washes his hands. "I am innocent of this man's blood," he says. "It is your responsibility!"

Finally, the hour has come.

The Lamb of God is about to be slain before the eyes of the world, but first the Roman soldiers decide to have some gruesome "fun" with Him.[5]

Jesus is flogged by a whip with multiple leather strips, each armed at the point with an angular bony hook or a sharp-sided cube. And after His captors have woven a crown from a thornbush, each thorn about an inch long and as sharp as a sewing needle, a soldier thrusts it onto Christ's head. Another man wraps a purple robe around His body, which by now looks like one big, open wound. The crowd then makes fun of Jesus, saying, "Hail, King of the Jews!"

As a final insult, they began to spit on Him and beat Him. The soldiers even play a little game with our Lord, demanding that He prophesy who would hit Him next as they punch Him in the face again and again and again.

Once Jesus reaches Golgotha (which means "the place of the skull"),[6] those who gather around the cross witness hate at its worst and love at its best. People so hate Him that they put Christ to death; God so loves them that He gives people life.[7]

---

5. See Matthew 27:27 MSG.
6. Matthew 27:33.
7. Mears, *What the Bible Is All About*, 435.

Iron spikes are driven completely through each of Christ's hands and feet. He is stripped naked and raised high into the air for everyone to see and mock as He hangs for hours in the intense Middle Eastern sun. Jesus eventually becomes so exhausted that no matter how hard He tries, He is not able to hold His body up by His pierced feet. He begins to hang from His torn hands, His weight slowly pulling His arms and shoulders from their sockets.

He struggles to keep shifting the strain back to His feet, but exhaustion eventually overtakes Him until, finally, He hangs completely by His arms. And it is at this moment that His body begins to slowly cave in on itself until He can't get enough air into His lungs.

And there, in the blistering heat—His body already swollen and bleeding from the floggings and beatings in the face, spikes driven through His hands and feet, bones popping out of His sockets—Jesus ever so slowly begins to suffocate to death.

Words prophesied hundreds of years earlier come to pass: "He was pierced for our transgressions, he was crushed for our iniquities; the punishment that brought us peace was on him, and by his wounds we are healed. We all, like sheep, have gone astray, each of us has turned to our own way; and the LORD has laid on him the iniquity of us all."[8]

→ HEAR HIM

Explore the Word: John 19:1–27

Ugly scenes! They're hard enough to write about, let alone to read and to ponder.

Remember what happened when the screws began to tighten on Pilate? The religious leaders labeled Jesus a threat to the country. "If you let this man go, you are no friend of Caesar. Anyone who claims to be king opposes

---

8. Isaiah 53:5–6.

Caesar."[9] That was hypocrisy at its best—or *worst*, rather. Not one of those Jewish leaders cared what Caesar thought.

Sadly, though, there are times in most of our lives when each one of us sells out to something—usually against our better judgment. Sometimes we opt for what's popular or what might advance a selfish desire. . .at the expense of truth. Maybe it's out-and-out denial of what's right as we observed earlier with Peter. Or maybe it's a case of going along with the crowd when we know we're making a wrong choice—as we just saw with Pilate. Whatever the case, most of us have done it.

It's usually an issue of *truth* versus *popularity*.

It's a tough spot to be in. But as we'll see with Peter, it's a dilemma that Jesus will constantly help us with. It's a position we find ourselves in that He will give us chance after chance to get right.

→ Know Him

• **God looks favorably upon those who set their minds to doing what's right, not what's popular.** Yet as author Henry T. Blackaby points out, the world won't always applaud our efforts to live on the side of truth: "At times, God will be the only witness to your righteous behavior. Sometimes God is the only one who will understand your motives. Sometimes you will do all you know God has asked you to do, only to face ridicule from others. At such times all you can do is maintain your integrity, trusting that God always keeps His eyes on you."[10]

> ✳ *Work It Out: What sins are clouding your judgment? Describe a time when you sold out to something that was popular (or seemingly enriching) instead of doing what was right.*

---

9. John 19:12.
10. Blackaby and Blackaby, *Experiencing God Day-by-Day* (Nashville: Broadman & Holman, 1998), 184.

• **A relationship in close communication with Jesus is the only way to live.** This relationship is dynamic, real, and personal. It is an invitation to a holy way of living. Jesus had an intimate relationship with the Father and He intends for us to know that we can be one in and with Him. This is the great invitation to be a holy people, not in our efforts, abilities, or energies, but in a death to self, so that He might live in us moment by moment. Without Him in this moment, nothing but darkness remains.

> ✳ *Work It Out: Describe in very practical ways exactly how a Christian can "abide" in Jesus. What about the internal "tug-of-war" between sin and holy living? How can we defeat temptation?*

• **Pray: "Lord Jesus—You are God. I love You and want to serve You."** Ask Him to help you live in truth. Ask Him to give you strength when you are tempted to compromise or give in to what's popular, not what's right.

→ NOTES FOR GROWTH

A Key Point I Learned Today:

_____

_____

_____

How I Want to Grow:

_____

_____

_____

My Prayer List:

_____

_____

_____

DAY 32:

THE CRIMINALS AND THE KING

Two other men, both criminals, were also led out
with him to be executed. When they came to the
place called the Skull, they crucified him there,
along with the criminals—one on his right,
the other on his left. Jesus said, "Father, forgive them,
for they do not know what they are doing."
And they divided up his clothes by casting lots.
— Luke 23:32–34

→ SEE HIM

Paradise Lost. . .and Found

Three rough-hewn wooden crosses stand starkly on a desolate hill. The ever-darkening sky sweeps down upon a mot-
ley crowd, painting an ominous backdrop to the rocky, arid
landscape.

Jesus hangs on a cross—with two criminals on each
side of Him.

People who pass along the road jeer, shaking their
heads in mock lament: "You bragged that You could tear
down the temple and then rebuild it in three days—so
show us Your stuff! Save Yourself! If You are really God's
Son, come down from that cross!"[1]

In the same way the chief priests, the teachers of the
law, and the elders mock Him: "He saved others," they shout,
"but He can't save himself! He's the King of Israel! Let Him
come down now from the cross, and we will believe in Him.

---

1. See Matthew 27:39–40, MSG.

He trusts in God. Let God rescue Him now if He wants Him, for He said, 'I am the Son of God.' "[2]

Even one of the criminals who hangs next to the Lord joins in the mockery. "Aren't You the Christ?" his voice croaks and wheezes. He gasps for air, wincing at the crushing weight upon his chest. "Save Yourself and us—if You can."

He knows death is imminent. The sticky blood that runs from his palms and the fluid in his throat serve as constant reminders. Sweat drips off his nose. His eyes roll back in his head like a crazy man's—yet he gathers enough hatred to focus them on the Man hanging beside him. "Even a son of the devil could call demons to save him," he says. "But You. . .are. . .nothing—"

"Enough!" snaps the other criminal. "Even in the face of death, you are a fool!" The man struggles to catch his breath. "Don't you get it? Don't you fear God? We are punished justly, for we are getting what our deeds deserve. But this Man has done nothing wrong."

As the second criminal glances at Jesus, tears begin to roll down his cheek.

A new weight has been pressing down on him, growing heavier as the day wears on. The nearer he comes to his end, the more rapidly the visions flow: victims, targets, innocents. Their faces haunt him now, each adding an unseen stone to the crushing weight of remorse. Yet as tormented as he feels, he somehow senses a greater weight upon Jesus. He'd heard the stories about Jesus—about healings and miracles. Hadn't He even stood up for the outcasts? Surely He did not belong here, dying between two notorious lawbreakers.

Is this really the Christ? Is God right there beside me, forgiving sin?

"Jesus," he sobs desperately. "Remember me when You come into Your kingdom!" His body slumps forward from

2. See Matthew 27:41–43, NIV.

the effort, and he feels the nails pinch and tear in his flesh.

Jesus' breath is labored also, but His reply is clear: "I tell you the truth, today you will be with Me in paradise."[3]

→ HEAR HIM

Explore the Word: Luke 23:32–43

Imagine how Christ's words of forgiveness reverberated deep into this man's soul. Love he had never known filled and cleansed him.

We, too, deserve to die for our sins. Yet how often are we like the first criminal? We do something wrong and find ourselves facing the consequences. We want Jesus to prove Himself, to save us from the situation we're in. We want Him to get us down off the cross, but we don't want to admit that we deserve to be there. Sometimes we even lash out at Jesus for the "injustice" we feel.

But like the second criminal, some of us choose to admit our sin, confess that Jesus is Lord—and receive the gift of eternal life. His story is a beautiful example of the power of confession. Casting aside pride, standing against shame, he submitted to Christ's authority.

Just as this criminal met his end with a peace certainly more powerful than death, so we can face our circumstances with strength, freedom, and guidance from God's Spirit.[4] Only when we make such a confession will we hear those exciting words from Jesus' lips, "You will be with me in paradise" (Luke 23:43).[5]

---

3. This story is adapted from Jeremy V. Jones, Greg Asimakoupoulos, and Michael Ross, *Tribe: A Warrior's Calling* (Colorado Springs: Focus on the Family, 2006), 129–31.

4. Ibid., 133.

5. Buursma, *Daylight Devotional Bible*, 1122.

→ KNOW HIM

• **Let go of pride.** While no one has escaped pride's grip, not many are willing to freely admit that they are guilty of this sin. Some people will confess other vices—a bad temper, a struggle with lust, an addiction—yet, somehow, a problem with pride is often overlooked. C. S. Lewis, on the other hand, challenges us to take pride very seriously. "The essential vice, the utmost evil, is pride. Unchastity, anger, greed, drunkenness, and all that, are mere flea bites in comparison: it was through pride that the devil became the devil: Pride leads to every other vice: it is the complete anti-god state of mind."[6]

> ✳ ***Work It Out:*** *C. S. Lewis describes pride as "spiritual cancer." Have you—or someone you know— been infected by it? (Describe what you observe and how you feel.) Has the presence of pride in your life blocked you from growing closer to God?*

• **Accept Jesus' invitation to a transformed life—for all eternity!** Reflect on these life-giving words from the apostle Paul (Colossians 1:21–23): "Once you were alienated from God and were enemies in your minds because of your evil behavior. But now he has reconciled you by Christ's physical body through death to present you holy in his sight, without blemish and free from accusation—if you continue in your faith, established and firm, and do not move from the hope held out in the gospel. This is the gospel that you heard and that has been proclaimed to every creature under heaven, and of which I, Paul, have become a servant."

> ✳ ***Work It Out:*** *Have you been real with Jesus and allowed Him to cleanse and free you from sin? (Read 1 John 1:9 and explain how this transforms a Christian's life. . .and helps us to grow spiritually.)*

---

6. C.S. Lewis, *Mere Christianity* (New York: HarperCollins, 2001), 121–22.

• Pray: "Lord Jesus, I confess my sin to You today. Please forgive me, purify me, and help me to grow closer to You." Thank God that He is faithful even when you are not. Ask Him to forgive you and to help you change your actions so you can live in a way that is pleasing to Him.

→ NOTES FOR GROWTH

A Key Point I Learned Today:

_____

_____

_____

How I Want to Grow:

_____

_____

_____

My Prayer List:

_____

_____

_____

DAY 33:

"WHY HAVE YOU
FORSAKEN ME?"

**At noon, darkness came over the whole land
until three in the afternoon. And at three in the
afternoon Jesus cried out in a loud voice,
"Eloi, Eloi, lema sabachthani?" (which means
"My God, my God, why have you forsaken me?").
— Mark 15:33–34**

→ SEE HIM

The Death of Jesus

Darkness. Silence. The world stands still for three long hours.

Some at the foot of the cross hear Jesus' cry and say, "He's calling for Elijah." (Perhaps "Eloi, Eloi" sounds like "Eli-yah, Eli-yah.")

One of the soldiers runs and gets a sponge dripping with sour wine, puts it on a stalk of a hyssop plant, and then lifts it so Jesus can drink.

Another says, "Leave Him alone. Let's see if Elijah comes to take Him down." Sarcasm? Probably. Yet there may be a deep-seated longing in this man's heart for a miracle—the hope for a supernatural rescue.

In reality, that rescue is happening for all of humanity. John the Baptizer got it right when he described Jesus as "the Lamb of God, who takes away the sin of the world!"[1] At this very moment, God is laying all of human sin on

---
1. John 1:29.

Jesus, and the last of the ancient prophecies are being fulfilled.

Jesus literally feels the physical torment and spiritual agony of the whole planet; every generation—past, present, and future. Yet despite the Lord's words of despair under persecution and divine rejection—God the Father has to turn His back on sin and, therefore, on His Son—Jesus clings to the victory of Psalm 22:30–31: "Posterity will serve him; future generations will be told about the Lord. They will proclaim his righteousness, declaring to a people yet unborn: He has done it!"

"It is finished," He gasps. "Father—into Your hands I commit My spirit."[2]

His body falls far forward, and His head sinks down between the wings of His rising arms. His long, wet hair falls over His head like a curtain.[3] He takes His last breath and dies.

At that moment, an earthquake rumbles the ground and the heavy temple curtain at the entrance of the Holy of Holies rips in two, top to bottom. Rocks are split in pieces. Tombs are opened up, and many bodies of believers asleep in their graves are raised. (After Jesus' resurrection, they leave the tombs, enter the holy city, and appear to many.)

The captain of the guard and those with him, when they see the earthquake and everything else that is happening, are scared to death. They say, "This has to be the Son of God!"[4]

→ Hear Him

Explore the Word: Mark 15:33–41

Onlookers witnessed even more than the fulfillment of prophecy during those hours. Nature itself began to cry out and writhe at what humanity was doing to its Creator. And

2. See Luke 23:46.
3. Wangerin, *Book of God,* 809.
4. See Matthew 27:45–54, MSG.

the captain was right. The barrier between the created and the Creator was destroyed—torn in two. Jesus' payment on the cross now made it possible for anybody to be pure enough to stand in God's presence.

God had paid for the world's disobedience. The sacrifice, the substitution for our punishment, was complete. We were freed from the deadly menace that taunted Adam and Eve and every human since.

Satan had lost. The war with sin was over!

Now it was simply up to each man, woman, and child to step forward and claim the victory that had already been won.

Now it is time to fight back.

Jesus once said, "This is war, and there is no neutral ground. If you're not on my side, you're the enemy; if you're not helping, you're making things worse."[5]

Where do you stand?

→ KNOW HIM

• **Accepting that we have a sinful nature can help us to remain humble and connected to the Savior.** Take a look at Charles Haddon Spurgeon's observations about the desperate state of the human heart. . .and God's forgiving, healing touch:

> *What a mass of hideous sickness Jesus must have seen. Yet He was not disgusted but patiently healed them all. What a variety of evils He must have seen. What sickening ulcers and festering sores. Yet He was prepared for every type of evil and was victorious over its every form. . . . In every corner of the field, He triumphed over evil and received honor from the delivered captives. He came, He saw, He conquered*

5. Luke 11:23 MSG.

*everywhere. . . . Whatever my case may be, the
beloved Physician can heal me. Whatever the state
of others whom I remember in prayer, I have hope in
Jesus that they will be healed. My child, my friend or
my dearest one, I have hope for each and all when I
remember the healing power of my Lord. In my own
situation, however severe my struggle with sin and
infirmities, I too may be of good cheer. He who on
earth walked the hospitals still dispenses His grace
and works wonders among His children. Let me
earnestly go to Him at once.*[6]

✳ ***Work It Out:*** *In what ways do you want Jesus to
heal you? Do you believe that He can do it? (Explain.)*

• **If all are broken, why do only a few admit it?** This is a
question worth pondering. The truth is, God doesn't expect
us to have it all together; it's okay to be broken. The Lord
is our Healer. He can accomplish in us what we cannot do
on our own. He will clean out all the junk that weighs us
down: our pride, our shame, our stubborn wills, our tendency,
as Paul wrote, to do "what I do not want to do."

✳ ***Work It Out:*** *What kind of "internal junk" is
weighing you down? (Be honest.)*

• **Pray: "God, in the Bible You've promised me a way of
escape from temptation so I can stand up under it. Please
show me that way right now."** Ask Jesus to give you clear
steps that you can begin taking that will help you break free
from the repeated struggles you face.

---

6. Charles Haddon Spurgeon, quoted in Calvin Miller, *The Book of Jesus* (New York: Simon & Schuster, 1996), 51–52.

→ NOTES FOR GROWTH

A Key Point I Learned Today:

_____

_____

_____

How I Want to Grow:

_____

_____

_____

My Prayer List:

_____

_____

_____

DAY 34:

RISEN FROM THE DEAD

The angel said to the women, "Do not be afraid, for I know that you are looking for Jesus, who was crucified. He is not here; he has risen, just as he said. Come and see the place where he lay. Then go quickly and tell his disciples: 'He has risen from the dead and is going ahead of you into Galilee. There you will see him.' Now I have told you."

— Matthew 28:5-7

→ SEE HIM

The Empty Tomb

Early Sunday morning, just before dawn, Mary Magdalene, Mary the mother of James, and Salome head to the tomb—their hearts breaking and their minds whirling with questions. They've come to anoint Jesus' body with more spices, but as they enter the graveyard, they receive the shock of their lives: Suddenly the earth reels and rocks under their feet as God's angel comes down from heaven—right up to where they are standing. He rolls back the stone and then sits on it. Shafts of lightning blaze from him. His garments shimmer snow-white.[1]

The guards are lying like dead men and the stone has been rolled away (see Matthew 28:1–11; Luke 24:10).

The angel seems to glow brighter and brighter, like white lightning. The women had already had enough to be startled about today, but the presence of this celestial being surely is the most frightening so far.[2] And the brightness

1. See Matthew 28:1–4, MSG.
2. Anderson, *Jesus*, 350.

of the angel is too much for them, so they look down and shield their eyes.

"Don't be frightened," the angel says. "And there's no need to be surprised. You're here looking for Jesus, but why do you look for the living in a tomb? He's not here. He's alive! Do you not remember that, back in Galilee, He told you He would be arrested and crucified and rise from the grave on the third day?"

"Come and see the place where He lay," the angel continues. "Then go quickly and tell His disciples: 'He has risen from the dead and is going ahead of you into Galilee. There you will see Him.' Now I have told you."

The women, deep in wonder and full of joy, lose no time leaving the tomb. They run to tell the disciples, but Jesus meets them along the way, stopping them in their tracks. "Greetings," He says.

They fall to their knees, clasp His feet, and worship Him.

"Do not be afraid," Jesus says. "Go and tell My brothers to go to Galilee; there they will see Me."

Meanwhile, the guards scatter. A few of them race to the chief priests with an incredible story about an earthquake at the tomb and an angel who rolled away the heavy stone. What do the chief priests do? They bribe the soldiers to lie. "Tell everyone that you fell asleep and that those disciples stole the body. Above all, don't even mention the earthquake and the angel!"

→ HEAR HIM

Explore the Word: Matthew 28:1–15

The resurrection was the proof, the seal of authenticity, that Jesus is who He claimed to be: the Son of God, the Messiah, the Savior—the King!

And here's what should make us all jump for joy: Jesus

destroyed the power of death and has given us eternal life. Your sinful nature, and mine, were crucified on the cross with Him. The "old you" died, and then Jesus raised up the "new you." As Christ-followers, we are no longer under the power of sin.

Jesus' death paid the price; His resurrection sets us free.

→ Know Him

• **Never try to mask sin.** Our specific sins are, and our sin nature is, a minute-by-minute reminder that the whole human race has the same disease. Not only does the Bible say, "All have sinned and fall short of the glory of God" (Romans 3:23), it also doesn't say, "All who come to faith don't sin and don't continue to need a Savior." Every one of us is stuck in the muck of our nature—just like Pilate who allowed the execution of an innocent man. . .and just like the chief priests who tried to cover up the truth when they discovered an empty tomb. Even as Christ-followers, too many of us pat ourselves on the back for "not sinning quite as much"—when, in reality, we've just learned to hide it better than those outside the household of faith.

> ✳ **Work It Out:** *What sins are clouding your judgment? List some steps you can take that will help you break free from these sins.*

• **Accept God's *free* gift of grace.** None of us deserves God's love and forgiveness. None of us deserves eternal salvation. We may *think* we deserve it, telling ourselves we've worked hard and "been good," but the truth is, the words *I deserve* don't enter into the grace equation. We don't earn grace, we don't sacrifice for it, and we don't work to get it. Likewise, even if we conclude we *don't* deserve grace on account of our bad behavior or persistent sins, we still get it. Grace isn't withheld from us just because we haven't met a certain standard. Grace depends entirely on one factor: Jesus' ultimate sacrifice. Jesus' death on the cross—the fact that He sacrificed His own life for each one of us—guarantees that we are forgiven again and again, loved abundantly by Him, and given eternal life.[3]

> ✳ **Work It Out:** *Does God's free gift of grace seem too good to be true? (Why or why not?) Have you ever thought that you are unacceptable in God's eyes? (Please explain.)*

• Pray: **"Lord Jesus—thank You for Your free gift of forgiveness, love, and salvation."** Ask Him to help you turn from sin daily and embrace the forgiveness He extends to all who call on Him.

→ NOTES FOR GROWTH

A Key Point I Learned Today:

_____

_____

_____

How I Want to Grow:

_____

_____

_____

My Prayer List:

_____

_____

_____

---

3. Portions of this section have been adapted from Arnie Cole and Michael Ross, *Tempted, Tested, True* (Minneapolis: Bethany House, 2013), 228, and was contributed by Michelle DeRusha.

DAY 35:

MIRACULOUS CATCH

He called out to them, "Friends, haven't you any fish?"
"No," they answered. He said, "Throw your net on
the right side of the boat and you will find some."
When they did, they were unable to haul the net
in because of the large number of fish.
—John 21:5–6

→ SEE HIM

Grief Turns to Joy

Peter doesn't feel like talking much.

He and the other disciples have cast off on the Sea of Galilee—doing their best to get on with their lives. At least the world of a fisherman makes sense: nets, lines, spears, mast, sail, oars—the smell of the salty water, the warmth of the sun on his back.

The small band of friends had just had their hearts ripped right out of their chests. Their Teacher, their Master—the one they believed to be the Messiah—had been nailed to a cross and executed. But as if that isn't horrible enough, Peter turned his back on Jesus.

"You are not one of His disciples, are you?" someone had asked him just hours before the crucifixion.

Fearing for his own life, he heard the ugly words roll quickly off his lips: *"I am not."*

But here's what Peter can barely stomach: he didn't just say this once, but three times! And upon his third denial, a rooster began to crow—just as Jesus had predicted.

So what hope is there for the man whose name means *rock*?

Suddenly, Peter hears that voice he'd come to trust—that comforting, irresistible voice. He looks up from the water and spots a man kneeling alone on the shore, trying to start a campfire. The guy is shouting at his crew, asking if they've caught anything yet.

"No," Peter yells back.

"Throw your net on the right side of the boat and you will find some."

What's the deal with this guy? Peter asks himself. *The last thing I need is some landlubber telling me how to do the one thing I know.*

Yet this man's voice seems strangely familiar. And when the guys do as the man instructs, the miraculous happens: they are unable to haul the net in because of the large number of fish.

"It's Him!" John is the first to realize the man is no stranger. And before he can say another word, Peter cannonballs into the water—clothes and all—leaving the rest of the guys to fight with the fish.

He splashes and strokes and swims as hard as he can—thankfully the boat is only a hundred yards from the shore. As he comes up out of the water, he can see every feature of the Lord's face. *It really is Him!*

Peter stands silently on the shore, feeling completely wretched and unworthy. *Why did I do it? How could I deny my Lord? When push came to shove, why did I crumble?*

Jesus has kindled a charcoal fire; bread and fish are already laid on it. Breakfast for one? Then Jesus looks past Peter and gazes at the other disciples, struggling to row their vessel and tow the heavy net shoreward. "Bring some of the fish you have just caught," He says.

Peter wades back into the water and helps drag the nets onto dry land. He and the other men spread out a wide carpet of glittering fish—all 153 of them.[1]

"Come and have breakfast," Jesus says.

---

1. See Wangerin, *Book of God*, 833.

The disciples know who He is by this time but are afraid to say anything. He serves them the bread and fish and they eat in silence.

→ HEAR HIM

Explore the Word: John 21:1–14

Can you imagine the tug-of-war of emotions Peter felt that morning? First hopelessness, then guilt and remorse, and finally heart-throbbing joy. But then one look at Jesus, and a firm tug on the "emotional rope" pulls him back into shame again.

As I (Michael) read this passage of scripture, one phrase comes to mind: *convertible Christ-follower.*

Think about it: Lots of gadgets in life are convertible—cars, clothing, computers, cooking utensils. With a tug and a snap, you can transform an open-air cruiser into a storm-proof sedan. . .or your handy laptop travel bag into the ultimate fast-paced workplace. But did it ever occur to you that Christians can be convertible, too? (Sadly, Peter gives us a prime example.)

The kinds of believers I'm describing act one way at church and at home, then transform into someone else when they're with the crowd. The Bible has a harsh way of describing convertible Christians: *hypocrisy.* Are you guilty of fake faith? Are you wandering through life with convertible convictions? If so, how can you reattach "authenticity" to your Christian walk?

→ KNOW HIM

• **Figure out what true conviction looks like.** It has been said, "A belief is what you hold; a conviction is what holds you." Yet a conviction is meaningless if it becomes convertible. A true conviction must include a commitment to live by what we claim we believe. So, for the sincere Christian, authentic faith is a consistent, unchanging resolution—a determined purpose to follow Jesus Christ and His teachings.

✴ ***Work It Out:*** *What happens to your convictions—your faith—when stress hits? (Keep in mind that a good way to sort real faith from the phony kind is to observe what happens when you're under pressure.) Are you consistently Christ's when the pressure hits. . .or do you crumble?*

• **Allow Christ to empower you.** Jesus Himself empowers us to live for Him. He gives us the strength to stay consistent and not fold into opineless hypocrites. (Of course, we have to put forth some effort.) We can be the same person at home, at work, at church. . .and with our friends. Christ gives us the strength. "Being confident of this, that he who began a good work in you will carry it on to completion until the day of Christ Jesus" (Philippians 1:6).

✴ ***Work It Out:*** *Like Peter, are you having trouble looking Christ in the eye? What's your first step toward mending your relationship with Him and breaking through sins like hypocrisy? (Hint: Flip over to James 5:16 for a clue.)*

• **Pray: "Jesus, help me break free from a phony faith."** Ask Him to reveal areas of your life that need work (sins to confess, habits to overcome, desires to commit to Him.) Ask Him to purge the old ways of thinking and acting— especially a lifestyle filled with envy, pride, anger, jealousy, lust, and confusion.

→ NOTES FOR GROWTH

A Key Point I Learned Today:

_____

_____

_____

How I Want to Grow:

_____

_____

_____

My Prayer List:

_____

_____

_____

JESUS IS "THE WAY,
THE TRUTH, AND THE LIFE"

DAY 36:

PETER GETS A
SECOND CHANCE

**When they had finished eating, Jesus said to Simon Peter,
"Simon son of John, do you love me more than these?"
"Yes, Lord," he said, "you know that I love you."
Jesus said, "Feed my lambs."
— John 21:15**

→ SEE HIM

A Tough Conversation about Faith—and Devotion

Jesus' question cuts deep: "Do you love Me more than these?"

Peter's mind is no doubt flashing back to his boastful claim in the Upper Room during the last supper: "Lord, I will lay down my life for you," he said impulsively during that touching moment.

And of course Jesus had known better. He countered with a dose of reality: "Will you really lay down your life for Me? I tell you the truth, before the rooster crows, you will disown Me three times!"

But as they sit by the Galilee shore and work toward reconciliation, Jesus is not only questioning Peter's devotion, but He's using the old name Peter had before He changed it. It's as if He's nudging Peter to start from scratch. It's as if He's wiping the slate clean. And Jesus doesn't just ask once if Peter loves Him; the Lord asks three times!

Peter's feelings are now hurt, and the floodgates of emotion burst free. He bows his head and begins to cry like a child. He can't raise his face to Him. "Lord," he says, "You know all things. You know that I love You."

Peter feels the Lord's hand on his shoulder. Jesus is kneeling in front of him. He crooks a finger beneath his chin and lifts his head. Peter looks through his tears and sees the Lord's eyes filled with such kindness that he bawls all the harder.[1]

"Then feed My sheep."

"The truth is, Simon," Jesus continues, "that as a young man, you are able to take care of yourself, be your own master. But you'll grow old and have to stretch out your hands. You'll need help to dress and you'll be taken places you won't want to go." Jesus is telling him obliquely how he will end his days and how in his death he will honor God.[2]

And then the Lord ends with an invitation He gave at the beginning: "Follow Me."

→ HEAR HIM

Explore the Word: John 21:15–25

Three times Peter denied Jesus in the high priest's courtyard. And three times Jesus had him confess his loyalty. It was a painful experience, but it was necessary to prove to the disciples and to Peter that he was back in the group, that Peter once again was assigned the task of looking out for others. It would not always be an easy job, but as long as Peter stayed humble and depended on God's power instead of his own ego, he would succeed.

Confession is the healing answer to a crippled walk.

You don't have to live with a huge load of guilt and shame in your life. Christ is reaching out to you with open arms—go to Him in prayer. Tell Him all about your sins, tell Him you're sorry, and He'll forgive you. "If we confess

1. Wangerin, 834.
2. *Book of God*, Templeton, *Jesus*, 194.

our sins, he is faithful and just and will forgive us our sins and purify us from all unrighteousness" (1 John 1:9).

Once you've confessed the sin and asked Jesus to help you change (called repentance), you can stop flogging yourself. You're completely forgiven. Now with your relationship fully restored with God, you can take steps toward growth and change. (The Holy Spirit will help you.)

Understand this: the Lord won't give up on you—even if it's the same sin you confessed yesterday. In Jesus, you'll find acceptance, love, and freedom—despite your shortcomings. Ask Him to go deep in your heart and to heal the real cause of what's making you stumble.

→ KNOW HIM

• **Undo untruth with truth.** At Back to the Bible, we get letters from Christians who struggle with all kinds of stuff: lustful thought lives, gossip, envy, jealousy, anger issues, addictions—the list goes on and on. Each person who writes me echoes the same desperate plea: "It's as if my problem is controlling me! I beg God to forgive me, and I even promise to stop doing what I don't want to do. But then I fail—again and again. Help!" In each case, the real problem usually isn't what a person thinks it is. Struggles with drugs or lust are almost always just the symptoms. The real problem is actually a heart problem. And the only way to fix a mixed-up, sin-filled heart is by having a daily truth encounter. That means spending time in the Word and in prayer, and in the fellowship of other believers.

＊ *Work It Out: Does it feel as if your faith is stuck? Are untruths clouding your judgment?*

• **Engage God's Word daily.** The Bible is more than just a bunch of letters printed on paper. Scripture is living and active. Above all, it's God-breathed. There is a supernatural component to the Bible that saturates our hearts and shapes our lives into what God wants them to be. Combine Bible reading with prayer and you've got a powerful weapon—an invisible sword, so to speak—that can fend off any deception and defeat *any* struggle that threatens to trap us.

> ✳ *Work It Out: During the past week, rate how often you have read the Bible: (1) daily, (2) a few times, (3) not at all. Do you think your consistency— or lack of it—relates to the health of your spiritual life. (Please explain.)*

• **Pray: "Lord, I want a right relationship with You. I confess my sins to You right now."** Don't hold back—tell Him everything. Tell Him how sorry you are, and thank Him for His forgiveness.

→ NOTES FOR GROWTH

A Key Point I Learned Today:

_____

_____

_____

How I Want to Grow:

_____

_____

_____

My Prayer List:

_____

_____

_____

DAY 37:
ON THE ROAD TO EMMAUS

When he was at the table with them, he took bread, gave thanks, broke it and began to give it to them. Then their eyes were opened and they recognized him, and he disappeared from their sight. They asked each other, "Were not our hearts burning within us while he talked with us on the road and opened the Scriptures to us?"
— Luke 24:30–32

→ SEE HIM

Jesus Walks with Two Travelers

On the same day Jesus arose from the tomb, two Christ-followers from the village of Emmaus decide to leave Jerusalem and head home. As they make the seven-mile trek, they talk openly about all that has taken place.

Jesus slips up next to them, disguised in some way.

He begins asking questions, testing them to see how much they understand about what has happened. The disciples stop in their tracks and stare at the disguised Christ. The expression on their faces is a mixture of sadness and incredulity.[1] One of them, named Cleopas, asks, "Are you only a visitor to Jerusalem and do not know the things that have happened there in these days?"

Jesus plays along. "What things?"

"About Jesus of Nazareth," they reply. "He was a prophet, powerful in word and deed before God and all the people." (Jesus probably winces at the description; they still don't get that He is the Son of God, the Light of the

1. Templeton, *Jesus*, 190.

World—the Lord and Savior of all!)

The one who was speaking continues: "The chief priests and our rulers handed Him over to be sentenced to death, and they crucified Him. But we had hoped that He was the One who was going to redeem Israel. And what is more, it is the third day since all this took place. In addition, some of our women amazed us. They went to the tomb early this morning but didn't find His body. They came and told us that they had seen a vision of angels, who said He was alive. Then some of our companions went to the tomb and found it just as the women had said, but Him they did not see."

Jesus finally sets them straight. "How foolish you are," He says, "and how slow of heart to believe all that the prophets have spoken! Did not the Christ have to suffer these things and then enter his glory?"

As they walk the rest of the way to Emmaus, He gives them a lesson in Old Testament quotations and stories that teach that the Messiah has to come and suffer for the sins of humanity. The two travelers are mesmerized by Jesus' teaching and want to hear more, so they invite Him to stay in Emmaus—not the usual courtesy invitation of hospitality but an impassioned plea to join them for dinner and spend the night.[2] "Stay with us, for it is nearly evening; the day is almost over."

Jesus agrees.

After washing up and settling down for dinner, the Lord conducts Himself like He is the host rather than the guest.[3] He takes the bread, breaks it in pieces for everyone at the meal, and speaks a prayer of thanksgiving. In a flash, they realize who He is.

He is indeed alive!

But even as it dawns on them, He is gone. They ask each other, "Were not our hearts burning within us while He talked with us on the road and opened the scriptures to us?"

---

2. Anderson, *Jesus*, 354.
3. Ibid.

They get up and return at once to Jerusalem. There they find the Eleven and those with them, assembled together and saying, "It is true! The Lord has risen and has appeared to Simon."

→ HEAR HIM

Explore the Word: Luke 24:13–35

Can you imagine their reactions when they realized that Jesus was right there beside them? Jaws dropped, hearts skipped a beat—feet jumped for joy! "It's Him—Jesus Christ! Our Lord and Savior risen from the dead! The hands—did you see the hands? Pierced. O my Lord, you're alive!"[4]

Now think about the hopelessness they experienced moments earlier.

At one time or another we each find ourselves on our own road to Emmaus—those long treks through grief, despair, disappointment, fear, worry, confusion. During those unsettling times, remind yourself of who's walking beside you. Trust that He has not abandoned you; hold tight to His promises in the Bible.

→ KNOW HIM

• **We can trust His Word when life feels out of control:**

—"The LORD is good, a refuge in times of trouble. He cares for those who trust in him" (Nahum 1:7).

—"Christ. . .suffered once for sins, the righteous for the unrighteous, to bring you to God" (1 Peter 3:18).

---

4. Buursma, *Daylight Devotional Bible*, 1124.

—"God so loved the world that he gave his one and only Son, that whoever believes in him shall not perish but have eternal life" (John 3:16).

—"Jesus said, 'Peace be with you! As the Father has sent me, I am sending you.' And with that he breathed on them and said, 'Receive the Holy Spirit' " (John 20:21–22).

—"This is love for God: to keep his commands. And his commands are not burdensome, for everyone born of God overcomes the world" (1 John 5:3–4).

✳ *Work It Out: Tell why you think it's important to study God's Word daily. What happens when you neglect the Bible?*

• **Let the Holy Spirit guide Yyou through the "Book of Hope."** Imagine having the Author of scripture teaching it to us, as He did with the two travelers on the road to Emmaus. It must have been incredible to walk side by side with Jesus, listening to Him teach and being able to ask Him questions. Now think about this: Back then, Jesus could only physically be in one place at one time. People had to go to that one place to reach Him. Today, however, everyone who has asked Him to be their Lord and Savior has the Holy Spirit inside—teaching and instructing them continually.

✳ *Work It Out: Why did Jesus choose to "open the scriptures" as He joined the two disciples on the road to Emmaus? (Why not just instantly reveal Himself?) Do you ever ask Jesus to guide you through the scriptures? (Explain what happens when you do this.)*

• Pray: "Lord, when life is hard, help me to remember that You have not abandoned me. Give me hope when everything else feels hopeless."

→ NOTES FOR GROWTH

A Key Point I Learned Today:

_____
_____
_____

How I Want to Grow:

_____
_____
_____

My Prayer List:

_____
_____
_____

DAY 38:

"YOU ARE WITNESSES"

He told them, "This is what is written: The Messiah
will suffer and rise from the dead on the third day,
and repentance for the forgiveness of sins will be preached
in his name to all nations, beginning at Jerusalem.
You are witnesses of these things. I am going to send you
what my Father has promised; but stay in the city until
you have been clothed with power from on high."
—Luke 24:46–49

→ See Him

Jesus Prepares the Disciples for Ministry

The two disciples Jesus talked to on the road to Emmaus
didn't waste a minute. They're back in Jerusalem, sharing
with the Eleven and other Christ-followers all that they
had encountered. As their story unfolds and they explain
how Jesus made Himself known when He broke bread,
the Lord suddenly appears in the room and stands among
them.

"Peace be with you," Jesus says.

Everyone is startled, thinking they are seeing a ghost.

"Don't be upset," He tells them, "and don't let all those
doubting questions take over." Jesus understands their fears,
and to prove to them that it's Him in the flesh—that He's
been physically resurrected from the dead—He stretches
out His hands toward them and pulls His robe aside so
they can see the wound in His side. "Look at My hands,
look at My feet—it's really Me. Touch Me. Look Me over

from head to toe. A ghost doesn't have muscle and bone like this."[1]

Still, the news seems too good to be true, and they're afraid to believe. Jesus again understands, and in His patience asks for some food to eat so they will know He has a physical body. Someone gives Him a piece of broiled fish. Jesus eats it.

"You'll remember," He says, "that when we were together earlier I impressed on you that every prophecy about Me in the Law of Moses, the Prophets, and the Psalms would have to be fulfilled. Let Me review it with you."

Then Jesus opens their minds so they can understand the scriptures. He begins another study, explaining how the Old Testament prophecies were fulfilled by His suffering for us. He goes on to explain that repentance for forgiveness of sins must be proclaimed to the whole world, starting right there in Jerusalem.

"This is what is written: The Christ will suffer and rise from the dead on the third day, and repentance and forgiveness of sins will be preached in His name to all nations, beginning at Jerusalem. You are witnesses of these things. I am going to send you what my Father has promised; but stay in the city until you have been clothed with power from on high."

→ HEAR HIM

Explore the Word: Luke 24:36–49

While our Savior's first call is "Come, follow me" (Matthew 4:19), His second is "Go"—"Go into all the world and preach the gospel to all creation" (Mark 16:15).

Yet exactly how are we to accomplish this? How can we get past the fear, take off the masks—and let people see the *real*, eternity-bound person inside? How can others

---

1. See Luke 24:36–41 MSG.

encounter the Savior through our lives?

God doesn't want you to hide your faith from the world. You're called to share the Good News. That could mean going next door and telling your neighbor about Jesus. . .or making Him known to your friends at school, or even within your own family. Let God's love shine through your life so others will come to Him. Christians aren't the ones missing out on good times—*the world is.*

→ KNOW HIM

• **Speak up**—instead of just being polite and keeping quiet. Maybe your friends don't seem too interested in spiritual issues right now, but get this: they're watching you, especially your faith. And if they come to you with a question one day, you need to speak up. "Always be prepared to give an answer to everyone who asks you to give the reason for the hope that you have" (1 Peter 3:15).

✳ *Work It Out: Share how you are going to speak up in the days ahead.*

• **Have some "backbone."** Matthew 22:37–39 tells us to love others, but that doesn't mean tolerating their sin. (Of course, it doesn't mean wagging your finger at them either or being self-righteous.) Sometimes the best way of loving a nonbeliever is with the word *no*—"No thanks, I don't smoke, drink, chew [insert the appropriate word]"—then letting your backbone do the witnessing for you. "Do your best to present yourself to God as one approved, a worker who does not need to be ashamed and who correctly handles the word of truth" (2 Timothy 2:15).

✳ *Work It Out: Share your plan for "pulling other up". . .without allowing yourself to be pulled down by sin.*

• Pray: "Lord, I want to be an 'approved worker' for God's kingdom." Ask Jesus to prepare you for service.

→ NOTES FOR GROWTH

A Key Point I Learned Today:

_____

_____

_____

How I Want to Grow:

_____

_____

_____

My Prayer List:

_____

_____

_____

DAY 39:

GET OFF YOUR "CAN'T" . . .AND GO!

"All authority in heaven and on earth has been given to me. Therefore go and make disciples of all nations, baptizing them in the name of the Father and of the Son and of the Holy Spirit, and teaching them to obey everything I have commanded you. And surely I am with you always, to the very end of the age."
—Matthew 28:18–20

→ SEE HIM

The Lord Commissions His Followers

Jesus' followers have just worshipped Him on the mountain near Galilee, and despite the fact that some disciples still have doubts in their hearts, Jesus commissions them and tells them to go out into the world.

"All authority in heaven and on earth has been given to Me," He tells them. "Therefore go and make disciples of all nations, baptizing them in the name of the Father and of the Son and of the Holy Spirit, and teaching them to obey everything I have commanded you."

As the Messiah lifts His hands to bless the disciples with the priestly benediction, the scars left by the nails are clearly visible.[1] As their eyes fall upon His nail-scarred feet, they are amazed to realize those feet are no longer touching the ground. As Jesus blesses them, He ascends into the sky,

1. Thomas Lancaster, *King of the Jews: Resurrecting the Jewish Jesus* (Littleton: First Fruits of Zion, 2006), 221.

rising to take His place as priest in the heavenly sanctuary.[2]

As He blesses them, He parts from them and is carried up into heaven.[3]

Finally the time comes for Him to leave, to go and prepare a place for His followers and to send the Holy Spirit. He rises up into the clouds with the promise that He'll return in exactly the same way (see Acts 1:9–11).

→ HEAR HIM

Explore the Word: Matthew 28:16–20

Jesus was a Man on a mission. From sunup to sundown He healed the sick, cast demons out of people, and proclaimed that the day of liberation had come—absolute freedom from fear, from worry, from bad thoughts, from bad actions, from bitterness, from grief—from chasing after what the world claims is important.

The Creator walked with His creation. And with Him came restored hope and healed hearts. Through His miracles, He told the world, "I am God, and I have brought you eternal life."

Jesus has commissioned us, too: "We are therefore Christ's ambassadors, as though God were making his appeal through us."[4]

The Lord didn't call us to hide in a Christian huddle—or to be part of His "secretive service." As Christians, we've grounded our lives on what the Bible says, which means we're convinced that humankind is more than just a cosmic accident. Jesus Christ is transforming our lives, and we've got to tell the world about it. Get this: those who don't know Christ are spiritually dead and are on their way to hell.

---

2. Ibid.
3. See Luke 24:51.
4. 2 Corinthians 5:20.

But as you've probably already discovered, your assignment to be a witness isn't easy. The Enemy hates for believers in Christ to become burdened for the world. He knows that they'll begin to pray, give, and even go to the ends of the earth to share the good news about Jesus Christ. So he'll do anything he can to divert our attention.

Keep in mind that Christ is greater than the Enemy. Christ has put the Holy Spirit inside of each Christian; and every minute of every day, if we let Him, He'll continue to teach, guide, protect, and, above all, love us and through us.

Are you willing to "get off your pew" and get going? If so, follow Christ's example and accept His call to "go" and "tell."

→ Know Him

• **Don't make witnessing so hard.** Too often, Christians fear they'll mess up in putting words to what God accomplished through the cross. We obsess over appearances and lose the purpose. We treat non-Christians like projects instead of people. We speak an alien language—known by insiders as "Christianese." The best thing we can do is relax and live what we believe, naturally, honestly, lovingly, and confidently. If we're not uncomfortable about our faith, non-Christians will have a better chance of seeing Jesus in us.

> ✳ *Work It Out: List people you can witness to. In the weeks ahead, pray for these people.*

• **Be confident with your faith.** We should never let fear hold us back from befriending unbelievers. Seek to create relationships with them. Consider the observations of legendary evangelist Billy Graham: "It is fear that makes us unwilling to listen to another's point of view, fear that our own ideas may be attacked. Jesus had no such fear, no such pettiness of viewpoint, no need to fence Himself off for His own protection. He knew the difference between graciousness and compromise and we would do well to learn from Him."

✳ *Work It Out: Are you ready with answers about your faith—why you believe what you believe? Has this book encouraged you? (As always, explain your answer.) In the days ahead, formulate answers to questions others may have about sin, salvation, and what Christ did on the cross.*

• **Pray: "Lord, give me a heart and a passion for evangelism."** Ask Jesus to open your ears and eyes to the lost and to show you to whom you should reach out. Ask Him to give you the courage and the words that will open their eyes to His love and grace.

→ NOTES FOR GROWTH

A Key Point I Learned Today:

_____

_____

_____

How I Want to Grow:

_____

_____

_____

My Prayer List:

_____

_____

_____

DAY 40:

WITH TONGUES LIKE FIRE

When the day of Pentecost came, they were all together in one place. Suddenly a sound like the blowing of a violent wind came from heaven and filled the whole house where they were sitting. They saw what seemed to be tongues of fire that separated and came to rest on each of them. All of them were filled with the Holy Spirit and began to speak in other tongues as the Spirit enabled them.

—Acts 2:1–4

→ SEE HIM

Filled with the Holy Spirit

Andrew is stunned by what he sees. He blinks a few times and refocuses. "It just can't be! Is this really happening?"

Right there in the packed room on Jerusalem's Upper Street, he and the other disciples are encountering something *super*natural. It begins with a sound like a violent wind. Then Andrew glances at his brother, Simon Peter, and sees something like a tongue of fire coming down on his head. And Simon begins speaking passionately, but in a language Andrew has never heard before.

Suddenly, the roar of the wind is not a sound anymore; it's a storm within his own soul, and Andrew is filled to bursting. He opens his mouth and begins to speak as enthusiastically as Simon, but in a different language altogether.

All the disciples have tongues of flame resting upon them. And all are speaking various languages. And foreign Jews who heard them yelling in their own foreign tongues have arrived to witness it. This is the Holy Spirit! Yes, this is power from on high, the promise of Jesus, and *that's* what Simon has been bellowing about.

Andrew's whole being "sings with the breathing of God."

When some people standing on the steps outside begin to make fun of them, saying that they're drunk, Peter shouts, "No! We are *not* drunk!" His booming voice silences the crowd. "You are witnessing what Joel prophesied long ago: God is pouring out His Spirit! As Joel said, 'In the last days, your sons and daughters will prophesy, your young men will see visions, your old men will dream dreams. Even on My servants, both men and women, I will pour out My Spirit in those days, and they will prophesy.'

"Listen to me," Simon Peter calls. "What you see and hear today—this is the work of Jesus! Repent and be baptized, every one of you, in the name of Jesus Christ for the forgiveness of your sins. And you will receive the gift of the Holy Spirit. The promise is for you and your children and for all who are far off—for all whom the Lord our God will call."

→ Hear Him

Explore the Word: Acts 2:1–21

Imagine being one of the disciples on that day. What would it have been like to feel that power surging through your body? It was probably the greatest feeling in the world!

What Peter shouted to the masses is true. If you've committed your heart to Jesus, then you share this experience, this supernatural, eternal "gift."

The Holy Spirit—the third Person of the Trinity—is our Guide, our Helper, our Strengthener, and our Advocate, sent to live in us and to control every aspect of our lives. Like the Father and the Son, God the Holy Spirit is to be believed and obeyed.

The first thing the Spirit will prompt you to do is speak about Jesus to others.

Empowered by the Holy Spirit, Peter took his heavenly assignment to heart. He stood before the Sanhedrin, the very men who would soon murder Stephen. It was Peter who later took the message of salvation to the Gentiles. Peter was the man whom King Herod imprisoned for his refusal to stop preaching the Good News, and then was miraculously freed by an angel. And it was Peter whose death, Jesus said, would "glorify God."[1]

God sent the Holy Spirit to fill our hearts so that we might sense His presence in our lives. Can you hear His voice directing your steps? Are you, like Peter, stepping out with power as Christ's witness?

→ Know Him

• **Be guided.** The Holy Spirit is a Counselor who lives in and with and all around us. Through His guidance, you can fulfill all the goals and plans God has for you. Call on Jesus for guidance in understanding God's message to you here and elsewhere in your life.

> ✳ *Work It Out: Share what God's assignment is for you right now. If you don't know, ask others to pray with you.*

• **Be encouraged.** The Spirit takes away fear—of rejection, of change, of failure—and gives hope and courage to face life's challenges. Jesus said, "You will receive power when the Holy Spirit comes on you; and you will be my witnesses."[2] In times of trouble—when things seem too hard

---

1. John 21:19.
2. Acts 1:8.

to handle—it is the Holy Spirit who is there to help you. Trust Him and know that He is your comfort and peace.

> ✳ *Work It Out: Share your fears, and discuss the possible roadblocks to fulfilling God's assignment for you. Ask others to pray with you about this as well.*

• **Pray: "Lord, fill me with the Holy Spirit."** Ask Him to draw you into His inner circle, helping you to know Him better. Ask the Lord to give you guidance and wisdom during times of turmoil *and* times of tranquility—during moments that involve big decisions *and* small ones.

→ NOTES FOR GROWTH

A Key Point I Learned Today:

_____

_____

_____

How I Want to Grow:

_____

_____

_____

My Prayer List:

_____

_____

_____